More Advance Praise for *Happiness Is Free*

"In his great book, *Happiness Is Free, and It's Easier Than You Think*, Hale Dwoskin continues the lifelong work and teachings of the great Lester Levenson, and has written a 'do-it-yourself', 'easier than you think,' Method that has transformed lives worldwide! With the information and exercises learned from this book, you will be able to let go of all that keeps you from living a life free from all limitations and live a life of happiness, joy and peace."

Diana Nightingale, Owner, Keys Publishing, Inc., international speaker, and author of *Learning To Fly As A Nightingale*

"*Happiness is Free* presents a psycho-spiritual perspective that applies the most esoteric wisdom to everyday human misery–and in a way that feels both practical and stunning, shows us how to move beyond insight and actually release what ails us. I am very grateful."

Nancy Dreyfus, Psy.D. author of *Talk To Me Like I'm Someone You Love: FlashCards for Real Life.*

"Stop Striving!! Learn to 'Let it Happen', not 'Make it Happen.' Hale and Lester, two 'master teachers' teach you a truly effortless way to a great life through the simple principles outlined in *Happiness Is Free*. These simple techniques can change your life–FOREVER! What we learned in a four-day class in 1991 has been concisely synthesized in this wonderful, instructional book. You will actually discover how to stop being your own strongest barrier to success. Within months of learning Lester's principles we began to reach personal, professional, and spiritual heights we had never known existed. We heartily recommend that you learn it for yourself. Because Happiness IS Free, and it really IS easier than you think."

Barbara Mark & Trudy Griswold, authors of *Angelspeake Trilogy and Heaven & Beyond: Conversations with Souls in Transition*

"In these times of turmoil and uncertainty, the simple yet profound truths expressed by Lester Levenson provide a powerful backdrop against which the events of our lives and our world can be seen and understood from an expanded perspective, bringing clarity and peacefulness in its wake. The commentaries provided by Hale Dwoskin help to build a bridge between the understanding of Lester's words and the organic integration of his wisdom into the day-to-day activities of our daily lives. For those already familiar with Lester's thoughts and with releasing, these volumes will bring additional depth and clarity to their understanding and practice. For those unfamiliar with Lester or his work, these volumes have the potential to be the doorway to a new way of looking at the world."

Elliott Grumer, Psychiatrist, Phoenix, AZ

Happiness Is Free

... and it's
easier than
you think!

Book 1

by Hale Dwoskin
& Lester Levenson

Sedona
Training Associates

Printed in the U.S.A. by Malloy Inc. on acid free 85% recycled paper.

Publisher:

Sedona Training Associates
60 Tortilla Drive, Suite 2
Sedona, AZ 86336
Phone: (928) 282-3522
Fax: (928) 203-0602
E-mail: release@sedona.com
Web: www.sedona.com

Cover design and illustration by Lightbourne © 2001
Interior book design by Wendy Barratt

Library of Congress Number:
ISBN 0-915721-00-7
Set of 5 books ISBN 0-915721-05-8
Special pre-publication limited edition.

To all seekers and finders

of the ultimate happiness everywhere

and Sedona Method® graduates

worldwide

Acknowledgments

I would like to thank the following people for making this book possible: My loving wife, Amy Edwards, all Sedona Method® graduates worldwide, Stephanie Gunning, Sara Whitcomb, Diane Brace, as well as all of the Sedona Training Associates staff.

Table of Contents

Lester Levenson

Happiness Is Free

. . . and it's easier than you think!

Book 1

Publisher's Note

If you have read any of the other books in this series, you will probably notice that the Introduction and How to Gain the Maximum Benefit from This Book sections are the same in each volume. This is done intentionally so that you can review them with each reading. If you have already read these chapters several times, you can choose to skip directly to the first session when exploring this book.

The Next Steps and Guidelines for *Happiness Is Free* Support Groups are also repeats. They are provided in this book for your convenient reference.

Introduction

What Is Happiness?

Quite simply put, happiness is you being your Self. Not the limited self that you pretend to be most of the time, but the unlimited Self that you are and have always been. This is the Self that is always effortlessly present before, during, and after everything else that appears in your experience. You are the radiant yet changeless background that allows for everything else to exist.

If that is true, you may be wondering, why is it so hard to discover and why have there been so many books written on the topic–including this one? The answer to that is not as simple.

We have spent eons pretending to be anything but unlimited. In fact, we have become so good at this pretending to be limited that we have forgotten that it is just a game, a pretense. We now spend most of our time bolstering the illusion that we have created for ourselves, leaving very little time for the inner reflection that can set us free from this totally self-imposed and artificial sense of limitation.

It takes tremendous energy to maintain the illusion that

unlimited Beingness is actually limited to the particular body-mind that you call yourself. No wonder we are so exhausted most of the time. We have unlimited energy available to us, but instead of using this energy for good or to discover who we truly are, we use this energy to convince ourselves and others around us that we are limited–that we have personal problems.

The late Lester Levenson, my friend and the coauthor of this book, used to say that extraditing ourselves from this situation in which we all find ourselves is either "simple or impossible." It is simple when we allow it to be easy. We can allow our energy to flow inwards towards self-discovery and for loving acceptance of what is. It is impossible when we force our energy to flow outwards. We fight against the world of our own creation and try to prove to everyone, including ourselves, that our world and its problems are real.

Are you ready to make it simple? You probably are if you were attracted to read this book. This book is designed to guide you experientially to rediscover your ultimate happiness by uncovering the real unlimited you.

The happiness that is you is totally independent of what you have or do not have, yet it improves your experience of whatever you have or don't have. This happiness that is you is also independent of what you do or do not do, yet it makes your experience of whatever you do or don't do more enjoyable. This happiness really is who you are, and you can experience it for yourself by reading this book and following the simple suggestions contained within it.

I know that you have probably heard promises like these before. And you may have often been disappointed. Which, of course, could make you a little skeptical. If you are in doubt, that is okay. I encourage you to believe nothing that you read in this book until you can prove it for yourself. But I promise you that this program is different. I have the absolute conviction that you can uncover your ultimate happiness and live it in every moment. This conviction is based on my own direct experience over the last quarter century of working with Lester Levenson and his teachings and then sharing them with thousands of people around the world.

Yet I did not always feel convinced. I met Lester Levenson in 1976. Back then I was an ardent, although confused seeker who had gone to many trainings and seminars led by teachers from both the East and the West. I had studied various body-centered disciplines, including Yoga, Tai Chi, and Shiatsu. I had actively participated in various courses, including EST, Actualism, Theta Seminars, and Rebirthing. I had many nice experiences at these seminars, and heard and understood—at least intellectually—many useful concepts. Still I felt incomplete. I longed for a simple and powerful answer to some important, yet vexing questions like: "What is my life's purpose?" "What is truth?" and "Who am I?"

Much of what I had heard and experienced only added to my questioning. No one seemed to have truly satisfying answers or have truly satisfied him or herself about what their true nature was or what was the ultimate truth. There was also a strong, almost universal belief that growing was hard work and required baring your soul and reliving painful, unresolved issues. However, that all changed during a very fortunate encounter with a remarkable man.

I met Lester at a seminar that I had organized for a well-known speaker, which Lester attended as the seminar leader's guest. That day, a group of us went out to lunch together, where Lester's presence immediately struck me as special. He was in total peace and equal-mindedness, very comfortable with himself. He was unassuming and easy to talk to, and treated everyone as his friend–even me, a complete stranger. It was obvious that he had ended his search by discovering the answers I'd been seeking. I knew I had to find out more.

When I asked Lester what he did, he invited me to a seminar that was being held the next weekend. All he would tell me about it was that, "a group of people is going to sit around a table and release." I wasn't sure what that meant, but I knew if it could even point me in the direction of the qualities of which Lester was the living embodiment, I definitely wanted it. I took a leap of faith and signed up on the spot.

Almost overnight I knew that I had found what I was looking for. In fact, deep inside I knew that this process of releasing and Lester's teachings were what I had been born to do and share with the world–and to this day I have never wavered.

Before we move on to explore more of what you can expect from this book, I would like to share Lester's story with you in his own words. The quote that follows is very similar to the story that Lester unfolded for me shortly after I met him and started exploring his teachings:

I was born July 19, 1909, in Elizabeth, New Jersey, into a middle class family as a very shy person. I tried to do things the way they were supposed to be done–doing the right thing, getting a good education, and being the best in my field. My natural inclination was towards science, especially the science of the world, and of man himself. I graduated from Rutgers University in 1931 as a physicist, after which I worked twenty-some years in physics and engineering.

In physics, I worked in research and development on measuring instruments and automatic control, connected with Brown Instrument Co., which later became a subsidiary of Honeywell. And in the engineering field, I worked as a mechanical engineer, an electrical engineer, a construction engineer, a heating and venting engineer, and a marine engineer–actually, fourteen different fields.

I also went into various businesses, including restaurants, lumber, building, and oil, intertwined with engineering, wanting to make money, wanting to make it in the world. At that time, I did not know what I now know–that what I was seeking was actually the answers to life itself. Nothing that I had worked at would give me that answer, and as the years went by, I became heavy with depression and with sickness.

By 1952, I had been through constant illness–I even had jaundice three or so times a year. I had an enlarged liver, kidney stones, spleen trouble, hyper- and hypo-acidity, ulcers that perforated and formed lesions, and to top it off, I had at least ten years of migraine headaches. This all culminated in 1952 when I had my second coronary thrombosis.

After the second coronary, I was told I would not live much longer–that I might die any day and shouldn't make the effort to take so much as a step unless I necessarily had to. I was extremely fearful of dying, but I said to myself, "You're still breathing, Lester–there is still a chance." So I sat down and began thinking on an "around the clock" basis. Having lived forty-two or so years, and having reached the end of the line without happiness, without health, I realized that all the knowledge I had accumulated was of no avail. I had studied Watson's behaviorism in the 30's and Freud's in the late 30's and early 40's. I had studied the philosophies. I had studied logic. I studied economics. I studied all the major fields of man, and with all that knowledge there, I was at the end of the line. This made me realize that the accumulated knowledge of man was of no use.

So I decided to start from scratch. Forget all that knowledge. Begin from point zero and see what you can pick up. So, I posed the questions, "What am I?" "What is this World?" "What is my relationship to it?" "What is Mind?" "What is Intelligence?" "What is Happiness?"

I began by asking myself, "What do I want out of life?" And the answer was happiness. Investigating further, I went into the moment when I was feeling happiest. I discovered something which to me was startling at the time. It was when I was loving that I was happiest. That happiness equated to my capacity to love rather than to being loved. That was a starting point.

I began correcting all my thoughts and feelings in that direction from that of wanting to be loved, to that of loving. And in that process, I discovered another major thing that kind of shocked me. I saw that I wanted to change this entire world, and that was the cause of my ulcers—or one of the major causes. In realizing how much I wanted to change things in this world, I saw how it made me a slave of this world, I made the decision to reverse that. And in the process of following out these two directions—actually unloading all the subconscious concepts and pressures in those directions—I discovered I was getting happier, freer, lighter, and feeling better in general.

As I saw this direction was good, I made the decision that if a slice of pie tasted this good, I wanted the whole pie. And I decided not to let go of this direction until I got that entire pie of happiness, and with it the answer to, "What am I? What is this life, and what is my relationship to it?" This decision allowed me, as I claim, to get the answer to life itself in a matter of only three months. I believe if I can do it, anyone can do it if they have that much "want to."

In that three-month period, all the ailments I had in my physical body corrected. All my miseries dropped away. And I ended up in a place in which I was happy all the time, without sorrow. Not that the world stopped pushing against me, it continued–but I was at a place where I could resolve things almost immediately. Having cleared out the negative fears, all the negative "I cannots," I would focus right on the answer to every problem, and get it very quickly. And so, my whole life turned around from being depressed and sick, to being happy all the time, and being in perfect health all the time.

One of the things that happened in this process was my identification with others. I saw that we are all related, we are all interconnected, each mind is like a radio broadcasting and receiving station; that we are all tuned into each other unconsciously–that we are just not aware of it. As a lot of the suppressed energies are let out, this becomes obvious to us and once we identify with everyone else it is just natural that we want everyone else to discover what we have discovered. That life was meant to be beautiful... meant to be happy all the time with no sorrow. And to be with perfect health. And so after reaching that high point of understanding in 1952, I have wanted to help others to discover what I had discovered.

I was deeply moved by Lester's story because it offered hope for all of us who may not have had the good fortune to have an ideal life. Lester was able to discover his true nature in a relatively short time and despite extreme adversity. If he could do it, I knew that I could, too.

The following quote is Lester expanding more about his actual realization:

I was at the end of my rope. I was told not to take a step unless I absolutely had to because there was a possibility that I could drop dead at any moment.

This was a terrible, shocking thing, suddenly to be told that I couldn't be active anymore, having been so active all my life. It was a horrible thing. An intense fear of dying overwhelmed me, the fear that I might drop dead any minute. This stayed with me for days. I went through a real, horrible, low, spinning period there, in the grip of intense fear of dying or of being a cripple for the rest of my life in that I wouldn't be able to be active. I felt that life would not be worthwhile any more.

This caused me to conclude with determination, "Either I get the answers, or I'll take me off this earth. No heart attack will do it!" I had a nice easy way to do it, too. I had morphine the doctors gave me for my kidney stone attacks.

After several days of this intense fear of dying, I suddenly realized, "Well, I'm still alive. As long as I'm alive there's hope. As long as I'm alive, maybe I can get out of this. What do I do?"

Well, I was always a smart boy, always made the honor roll. Even got myself a four-year scholarship to Rutgers University at a time when scholarships were very rare through competitive examinations. But what does this avail me? Nothing! Here I am with all this brilliance, as miserable and scared as can be.

Then I said, "Lester, you were not only not smart, you were

Dumb! Dumb! Dumb! There's something wrong in your intellect. With all your knowledge, you've come to this bottom end! Drop all this knowledge you've so studiously picked up on philosophy, psychology, social science, and economics! It is of no avail! Start from scratch. Begin all over again your search for the answers.

And with an extreme desperation and intense wanting out—not wanting to die, I began to question, "What am I? What is this world? What is my relationship to it? What do I want from it?"

"Happiness."

"Well, what is happiness?"

"Being loved."

"But I am loved. I know several very desirable girls with beauty, charm, and intellect who want me. And I have the esteem of my friends. Yet, I'm miserable!"

I sensed that the closest thing related to happiness was love. So I began reviewing and reliving my past love affairs, looking at the points where the little happiness that I had were. I began to pull up and dissect all my high moments of loving. Suddenly, I got an inkling that it was when I was loving that I had the highest feeling!

I remembered one evening, a beautiful balmy evening in the mountains when I was camping with my girlfriend. We were both lying on the grass, both looking up at the sky, and I had my arm around her. The nirvana, the perfection of the height of happiness was right there. I was feeling how great is love for my girlfriend! How wonderful is knowing all this nature! How perfect a setting!

Then I saw that it was my loving her that was the cause of this happiness! Not the beauty of the setting or being with my girlfriend.

Then I immediately turned to the other side. Boy it was great when she loved me! I remembered the moment when publicly this beautiful, charming girl told the world that she approved of Lester, she loved Lester–and I could feel that nice feeling of approval. But I sensed that it was not as great as what I had just discovered. It was not a lasting feeling. It was just for the moment. In order for me to have that feeling continuously, she had to continue saying that.

So, this momentary ego approval was not as great as the feeling of loving her! As long as I was loving her, I felt so happy. But when she loved me, there were only moments of happiness when she gave me approval.

Days of further cogitation gradually revealed to me that this was correct! I was happier when I loved her than I was when I got that momentary ego-satisfaction when she loved me. Her loving me was a momentary pleasure that needed constant showing and proving on her part, while my loving her was a constant happiness, as long as I was loving her.

I concluded that my happiness equated to my loving! If I could increase my loving, then I could increase my happiness! This was the first inkling I had as to what brings about happiness. And it was a tremendous thing because I hadn't had happiness. And I said, "Gee, if this is the key to happiness, I've got the greatest!" Even the hope of getting more and more happiness was a tremendous thing, because this was the number one thing I wanted–happiness.

That started me on weeks and weeks of reviewing my past love affairs. I dug up from the past, incident after incident when I thought I was loving, and I discovered that I was being nice to my girlfriends, trying to get them to love me, and that that was selfish. That was not really love. That was just wanting my ego bolstered!

I kept reviewing incidents from the past, and where I saw that I was not loving, I would change that feeling to loving that person.

Instead of wanting them to do something for me, I would change it to my wanting to do something for them. I kept this up until I couldn't find any more incidents to work on.

This insight on love, seeing that happiness was determined by my capacity to love, was a tremendous insight. It began to free me, and any bit of freedom when you're plagued feels so good. I knew that I was in the right direction. I had gotten hold of a link of the chain of happiness and was determined not to let go until I had the entire chain.

I felt a greater freedom. There was an easier concentration of my mind because of it. And I began to look better at my mind. What is my mind? What is intelligence?

Suddenly, a picture flashed of amusement park bumper-cars that are difficult to steer so that they continually bump into each other. They all get their electrical energy from the wire screen above the cars through a pole coming down to every car.

The power above was symbolic of the overall intelligence and energy of the universe coming down the pole to me and everyone else, and to the degree we step on the gas do we use it. Each driver of the cars is taking the amount of energy and intelligence that he wants from that wire, but he steers his car blindly and bumps into other cars, and bumps and bumps.

I saw that if I chose to, I could take more and more of that over-all intelligence.

And so I dug into that. I began to examine thinking and its relationship to what was happening. And it was revealed that everything that was happening had a prior thought behind it and that I never before related the thought and the happening because of the element of time between the two.

When I saw that everything that was happening to me had a thought of it before it happened, I realized that if I could grab hold of this, I could consciously determine everything that was happening to me!

And above all, I saw that I was responsible for everything that had happened to me, formerly thinking that the world was abusing me! I saw that my whole past life, and all that tremendous effort to make money and in the end, failing, was due only to my thinking!

This was a tremendous piece of freedom, to think that I was not a victim of this world, that it lay within my power to arrange the world the way I wanted it to be, that rather than being an effect of it, I could now be at cause over it and arrange it the way I would like it to be!

That was a tremendous realization, a tremendous feeling of freedom!

I was so ill when I started my searching; I had one foot in the grave. And when I saw that my thinking was cause for what was happening to me, I immediately saw my body from my chin down to my toes as perfect. And instantly, I knew it was perfect! I knew the lesions and adhesions of my intestine due to perforated ulcers were undone. I knew everything within me was in perfect running order.

And it was.

Discovering that my happiness equated to my loving, discovering that my thinking was the cause of things happening to me in my life gave me more and more freedom. Freedom from unconscious compulsions that I had to work, I had to make money, and I had to have girls. Freedom in the feeling that I was now able to determine my destiny, I was now able to control my world, I was now able to arrange my environment to suit me. This new freedom lightened my internal burden so greatly that I felt that I had no need to do anything.

Plus, the new happiness I was experiencing was so great! I was experiencing a joy that I had never known existed. I had never dreamed happiness could be so great.

I determined "If this is so great, I'm not going to let go of it until I carry it all the way!" I had no idea how joyous a person could be.

So, I began digging further on how to extend this joy. I began further changing my attitudes on love. I would imagine the girl I wanted most marrying one of my friends, or the boy I would want her to marry least, and then enjoy their enjoying each other. To me, this was the extreme in loving, and if I could achieve it, it would give me more of this wonderful thing that I was experiencing.

And so I worked on it. I took a particular fellow, Burl, and a particular girl, and I wouldn't let go until I could really feel the joy of their enjoying each other.

Then I knew I had it–or almost had it.

Then later on, I had further tests of this in talking to people who were opposing me no end when I was trying to help them. I would consciously feel the greatest love for them when they were attacking me. And the joy of loving them was so wonderful, I would, without any thought, thank them so profusely for having given me the opportunity of talking with them, that it threw them into a dither.

But I really felt that. I thanked them from the bottom of my heart for having given me the opportunity of loving them when they were making it as difficult as they possibly could. I didn't express that to them. I just thanked them for the opportunity of having been able to talk with them.

That I was able to do this was good news to me because, like other things, I was able to carry loving to the extreme. I could love people who were opposing me.

And I would not stop until I could see the end of the line of this happiness I was getting. I would go higher and higher and higher and say, "Oh, my gosh, there can be nothing higher than this!" But I would try. And, I would go higher. Then I would say, "Oh, there can't be anything higher than this!" But I would try, and go higher! And then say, "Oh, there can't be anything happier than this!" until I realized there was no limit to happiness!

I would get incapacitated. I could look at my body, and I couldn't move it I was so top-heavy with ecstasy and joy. I was actually incapacitated. I would do this for hours, going higher and higher and then I would have to work for hours to keep coming down and down and down until I could start being the body again in order to operate it.

Contemplating the source of intelligence and energy, I discovered that energy, as well as intelligence was available in unlimited amounts, and that it came simply by my freeing myself from all compulsions, inhibitions, entanglements, hang-ups. I saw that I had dammed up this energy, this power, and all I had to do was pry loose the logs of the dam which were my compulsions and hang-ups—and that was what I did. As I let go of these things, I was removing logs and allowing this infinite energy to flow, just like a water dam flows if you pull the logs out, one by one. The more logs you pull out, the greater the flow. All I needed to do was to remove these logs and let the infinite power and energy flow.

Seeing this, the power that was right behind my mind was allowed to flow through like it had never flowed before. There were times when I'd get this realization of what I am that would put so much energy into me, I would just jump up in the air from my chair. I would go right straight out the front door, and I would start walking and walking and walking, for hours at a time–sometimes for days at a time! I just felt as though my body would not contain it, that I had to walk or run some of it off. I remember walking the streets of New York City in the wee hours of the morning, just walking at a very good pace, and not being able to do anything otherwise! I had to expend some of that energy. It was so tremendous.

I saw that the source of all this energy, of all intelligence was basically harmonious, and that harmony was the rule of the universe. And that was why the planets were not colliding, and that was why the sun rose every day, and that was why everything functioned.

When I started my search, I was a very convinced and absolute materialist. The only thing that was real was that which you could feel and touch. My understanding of the world was as solid as concrete. And when some of these revelations came to me that the world was just a result of my mind, that thinking determined all matter, that matter had no intelligence, and that our intelligence determined all matter and everything about it. When I saw that the solidity that I formerly had was only a thought itself, my nice, solid, concrete foundations began to crack. Twenty years of buildup began to tumble.

And my body shook, and shook so much; I just shook for days. I shook just like a nervous old person. I knew that the concrete view I had had of the world was never going to be again. But it didn't drop away gracefully, with ease. For days, I actually shook, until I think I shook the whole thing loose.

Then, my view was just the opposite of what it had been

months previously, that the real solid thing was not the physical world, was not my mind, but something, that was much greater. The very essence, the very Beingness of me was the reality. It had no limits, it was eternal, and all the things that I saw before were the least of me, rather than the all of me. The all of me was by Beingness.

I saw that the only limitations I had were the ones that I accepted. So, wanting to know what am I? And looking for this unlimited Being that I had had an inkling of, I got insight of this tremendous unlimited Being that I am.

And on seeing that, I right there and then realized, "Well, I'm not this limited body and I thought I was! I am not this mind with its limitations that I thought I was!"

And I undid all body limitation, and almost all mind limitation, just by saying, "I am not it! Finished! Done! Period! That's it!" I so declared.

It was obvious to me that I wasn't that body and mind that I had thought I was. I just saw that's all! It's simple when you see it.

I let go of identifying with this body. And when I did that, I saw that my Beingness was all Beingness. That Beingness is like one grand ocean. It's not chopped up into parts called drops of bodies. It's all one ocean.

This caused me to identify with every being, every person and even every atom in this universe. Then you are finished forever with separation and all the hellishness that's caused only by separation.

Then you can no more be fooled by the apparent limitations of the world. You see them as a dream, as an appearancy, because you know that your very own Beingness has no limits.

In reality, the only thing that is, is Beingness. That is the real, changeless substance behind everything.

Everything of life itself was open to me, the total understanding of it. It is simply that we are infinite beings, over which we have superimposed concepts of limitation (the logs of the dam). And we are smarting under these limitations that we accept for ourselves as though they are real, because they are opposed to our basic nature of total freedom.

Life before and after my realization was at two different extremes. Before, it was just extreme depression, intense misery, and sickness. After, it was a happiness and serenity that's indescribable. Life became so beautiful and so harmonious that all day, every day, everything would fall perfectly into line.

As I would drive through New York City, I would rarely hit a red light. When I would go to park my car, people, sometimes two or three people, would stop and even step into the street to help direct me into a parking space. There were times when taxi cab drivers would see me looking for a parking space and would give up their space for me. And after they did, they couldn't understand why they had done it. There they were, double-parked!

Even policemen who were parked would move out and give me their parking place. And again, after they did, they couldn't understand why. But I knew they felt good in doing so. And they would continue to help me.

If I went into a store, the salesman would happily go out of his way to help me. Or, if I would order something in a restaurant and then change my mind, the waitress would bring what I wanted, even though I hadn't told her.

Actually everyone moves to serve you as you just float around. When you are in tune and you have a thought, every atom in the universe moves to fulfill your thought. And this is true.

Being in harmony is such a delightful, delectable state, not because things are coming your way, but because of the feeling of God-in-operation. It's a tremendous feeling; you just can't imagine how great it is. It is such a delight when you're in tune, in harmony—you see God everywhere! You're watching God in operation. And that is what you enjoy, rather than the time, the incident, the happening. His operation is the ultimate.

When we get in tune, our capacity to love is so extreme that we love everyone with an extreme intensity that makes living the most delightful it could ever be.

When I found the quote above I was deeply moved, and as I worked to put this book together I knew it was important for you to be exposed to it as well so you could appreciate the point of view from which Lester did his teaching.

Lester dedicated the rest of his life, from 1952 through his death in 1994, as he put it, to "helping the rest of him discover what he had discovered." He joyously lived for others without any sense of sacrifice, tirelessly working to help them to discover their true nature or at least let go of their suffering. Despite his best intentions he was not always understood. He used to say, "You only hear ten percent of what I say." Which, in my experience working with him and watching how others related to him, was quite generous. In fact, the very people that he helped the most often vehemently opposed him. But this never deterred him, nor did it ever shake his unqualified happiness and peace.

He worked with people on a one-to-one basis and in small groups, teaching sessions very much like those you will experience in this book. Until, around 1974, with the help of some of his closest students, he summarized his teaching into a do-it-yourself system that we now call the Sedona Method®. He did this to take himself out of the teaching loop. No matter how often he protested to the contrary, his students would often attribute their gains and realizations to him because they felt so elevated in his presence. He wanted everyone to know that they could discover just what he had on their own without needing an external teacher.

As you read this book and work with the material contained with in it, you will have a direct experience of Lester's teaching style through his words and their import. This is significant because it is something that very few people were lucky enough to experience during the last twenty years of his life. You will also have the benefit of seeing how his teachings have evolved since the creation of the Sedona Method® and in the work of his students since his passing.

Before Lester died, he asked me to continue his work and to continue to find ways to make the experience of letting go more readily available to those who are interested. That is why I have added some commentary and suggestions at the end of each session. I hope you will find these as helpful as I did.

I urge you to treat this book as a home study course in discovering your true nature and uncovering your innate happiness. You can benefit from this book even if you only read it casually. But if you dedicate yourself to using it to the fullest, the results you can achieve will astound you.

How to Gain the Maximum Benefit from This Book

A Seven-week Course on Liberating the Happiness, Peace, and Joy Within

This book is designed to be a seven-week home study course on the ultimate happiness. Read and work with one chapter per week. Each chapter contains a session from Lester along with my comments and suggestions to help you understand his message, as well as space for note and realizations. However, I would suggest that you do your best to get the most out of Lester's words in each session before moving on to the commentary. You may need to allow some extra time to sit with each paragraph or the whole session. You may also want to revisit the chapter repeatedly throughout the week.

You Have All the Time in the World

We live in an incredibly fast paced world where we are constantly forcing ourselves to move more rapidly in order just to keep up. In our rush to attain our goals, especially in the spiritual realm, we are often rushing past the very moment that offers the greatest opportunity for self-recognition–now. If you read this book in a hurry you may find you get what Lester used to call "spiritual indigestion." Therefore, I highly encourage you to read this material and approach it as an exploration of life as though you have all the time in the world.

Don't Believe Anything We Say

Especially with spiritual teachers, there is a tendency simply to accept what they say on hearsay or belief. Lester strongly felt that we should avoid doing this with any teacher. Instead we should allow ourselves to stay open to a teacher's message as an exploration or an experiment in consciousness. We should only accept what he or she teaches once we can prove it for ourselves through our own experience. Lester used to call this "taking it for checking."

I suggest that you take everything that you are exposed to in this book for checking. Allow yourself to be as open to the message as you can without accepting it on blind faith. You will find that this material has much more value for you when you explore it in your own life.

On the other hand, I also highly recommend that you suspend comparison and judgment as best you can. You may find that some of what you are exposed to in this book contradicts what you have learned from other teachers. I would suggest that you do not throw out the other material that you have learned, but merely put it aside as best you can while you explore these sessions. Once you have had time to draw your own conclusions, then you can go back and compare this material to everything else you have learned and see where it fits.

Contradiction is inevitable when you compare different paths or traditions of growth. However, this does not invalidate the different points of view. What every good teacher does is speak to the audience at hand to the best of their ability. Sometimes they may appear to contradict themselves because each audience they address needs to experience the teachings from different levels or perspectives. For this reason you may even notice apparent contradictions between me and Lester and Lester and himself. Contradiction can be most palpable when you compare different teachers. Not only are they speaking to different audiences, they are also bringing their own unique perspective to the topic–as they should be.

When it comes to truth, if you can allow yourself to embrace all possibilities you will find yourself understanding and applying the wisdom you gain on a much more useful, deeper, and heartfelt level. There are many rays that lead to the one sun.

It Is a Matter of Resonance

From my perspective, everything in the world has its own vibration or resonance, including you and everyone you meet. Have you ever noticed that some people tend to pull you up when you are with them and others seem to pull you down, and that they often don't need to say or do anything to have this effect on you? As we grow in understanding on the path, our resonance or frequency tends to go up. But it is not just a matter of higher or lower. We all relate better with some people than others, even if they are on the same level of vibration as us. Of course the same thing is true for teachers.

As you read this material, you may find that you resonate intensely with certain statements while others leave you feeling blank or unmoved. Lester recommended that you highlight the chapters, phrases, or statements that move you most for future reference, then go back and spend some time pondering them. Over time, as you revisit this material, other parts of it will stand out more than they did initially. That is because you will have changed and become ready to see things from a new perspective. When this happens, allow yourself to honor the change and shift your focus accordingly.

About Lester's Language

Lester had a unique way of using the English language. I have purposely preserved his style of communication because I've noticed that when you read or listen to any teacher in his or her own vernacular, the words have more of an import than when they have been heavily edited. My intention here is to give you the feel of having been present as Lester's talks unfolded, so that you can be as open as possible to his deepest message.

Lester came to this unique communication style for several reasons. His realization came quickly and spontaneously without him following any particular teacher or discipline or even having done any reading or studying of the path. Thus he had no language that adequately expressed what he was experiencing and what he wanted to share with others. As a result he looked in existing spiritual books from both the East and the West to try and find a suitable language that would best communicate his amazing discoveries. From the East, he was attracted to the teachings and writings of Ramana Maharshi and Paramahansa Yogananda. From the West, he drew upon the Bible, especially the New Testament. You will probably notice the influence of these sources in his writing. Occasionally he even slips into old English to express himself.

Most of the Lester material in this book comes from talks that took place in the 1960's and early 1970's. Therefore he often uses a vernacular that was more appropriate for that era. You will notice that his reference to current events and things like population figures are also reflective of that same time period.

In addition, Lester had difficulty grounding himself in time. He saw time as a self-imposed limitation or merely a concept. He would refer to things as happening yesterday that happened ten or twenty years earlier, and things that were about to happen that have yet to occur. He always seemed to be factually accurate and yet frequently was not able to place his perceptions in the appropriate time period.

Lester also did not believe in the limitation of space, so here and there often had the same meaning to him. He would often refer to getting "there" when referring to Beingness when he really meant "here." Or "going free" when he knew there was nowhere to go. He also used language this way because he was wanting to communicate to people where they were. Most people believe that Beingness is apart from where they are now. That's why they go looking for it. The "there" that Lester referred to when speaking of Beingness is closer than your breath.

Lester also learned his instructing style from an old school that uses imperatives heavily. He often used the charged words "should," "have to," "must," and "only." These charged words were often used by Lester to wake people up by using a little extra force. If you notice that these words stir up resistance in you, this in normal. These words tend to do that in most of us. Allow yourself to let go of the resistance as best you can and be open to the under-lying message.

Please keep these points in mind as you read the sessions so you can allow yourself to remain as open as possible to his message with-out getting lost in how it is being communicated.

When Two or More Are Gathered in Thy Name

The exercises that follow each session have been or will be explored as part of the advanced courses we teach at Sedona Training Associates. They are designed so that you can benefit from either doing them on your own or sharing them with a friend, rela-tive, or loved one. There is an awesome power that is unleashed when we gather together to focus on truth. That is why Sedona Training Associates hosts live seminars to explore this topic and why you can benefit from sharing this material with others.

If you choose to do the exercises at the end of each session with someone else, you can ask each other the questions or lead each other in the explorations. All you need to do is be as present as you can with your partner and ask them the questions in the third per-son using the pronoun "you" instead of "I." Grant your partner their Beingness by allowing them to have their own exploration.

When you are asking your partner to let go, do your best to let go as you facilitate your partner in releasing. You will find that this happens naturally if you are open to it. Refrain from leading, judging their responses, or giving them advice. Also refrain from discussing the explorations until you have both completed them during that sitting and you mutually agree to discuss them. Also validate your partner's point of view even if it does not agree with your own.

Please refrain from playing the role of counselor or therapist unless you're a trained counselor or therapist and have been specifically asked by your partner to play this role with them. Also, if they bring up a medical condition that would ordinarily require a trained medical professional, suggest that they get whatever support they need in this area. If you are not sure whether or not they truly need medical support, you can suggest it anyhow, just to be sure.

Write Down Your Gains

As you move diligently through this material, you will find that it has many powerful positive effects on you. We call the changes that come from this exploration "gains," and I highly recommend that you write them down, as they occur, to spur you on to even greater self-discovery.

The following is a list of some gains you can expect as you work with this book:

- Positive changes in behavior and/or attitude
- Greater ease, effectiveness, and joy in daily activities
- More open and effective communications
- Increased problem solving ability
- Greater flexibility
- More relaxed and confident in action
- Accomplishments
- Completions
- New beginnings
- Acquiring new abilities or skills
- Increase in positive feelings
- Decrease in negative feelings
- More love towards all beings

As you read and explore this material you will also have realizations about your own patterns of limitation and realizations about the nature of Reality itself. I highly recommend that you write these down as well.

There are seven blank pages at the end of each session, one for each day of the week, which are designed for you to write down your gains and realizations.

Be Open to the Unexpected

Realizations and gains definitely will come as you consciously work with this material, however, they will also come when you least expect them. Often it is when we are not looking for, or trying to accomplish anything that the mind relaxes enough to allow realization. So make room for this possibility throughout your day. As best you can, relax and accept that the timing of your greatest breakthroughs and realizations, including the ultimate realization of your true nature, may be totally out of your control.

It Is All a Matter of Letting Go or Releasing

Lester strongly believed that growing on the path was a function of your willingness, ability, and follow-through in letting go. He was so adamant about this point that he dedicated the last twenty years of his life solely to this one aspect of his teachings and encouraged the development and practice of what we now call the Sedona Method®. To get the most from this book, I highly recommend that you learn the Sedona Method® and practice it as you read and work with Lester's material. Even if you don't, I highly encourage you to do some form of letting go in order to deal with whatever this material invariably brings up into your consciousness.

You will get the most out of it if you allow yourself to let go as best you can.

To this end, I will be making suggestions throughout the book of what and how to let go as you explore what Lester has to offer. I have also included the following guidelines on releasing so that you can start to apply this technique in your life as you study this course in the ultimate happiness.

Holistic Releasing™

Holistic Releasing™ is the latest advancement in the continuing improvement and development of the process that we at Sedona Training Associates call letting go, releasing, or the Sedona Method®. If you've worked with us before, you're aware that in our Sedona Method® classes and taped programs we mainly focus on three methods of letting go. The first is letting go by choosing or making a decision just to drop whatever we're holding onto in the present moment. The second is letting go by allowing whatever is to be in this moment, welcoming it fully and seeing it almost like the clouds that pass through the sky, needing no correction, no changing, no fixing. The third way is letting go by diving into the very core of whatever the feeling is. When we dive into the very core of any feeling, we discover that it's empty inside–or full of goodness–not full of the darkness that we generally assume will be there.

I recently developed a fourth way of letting go that we call Holistic Releasing™. This process is what many of the suggestions at the end of each chapter are all about. It has two purposes. If you've worked with the Sedona Method® before, it's a way of deepening the work that you're already doing. And if you haven't worked with the Sedona Method® before, it's a way to open your understanding of the whole process of letting go. It is a way of having whatever you want in life.

The Holistic Releasing™ process will help you to collapse, dissolve, or let go of whatever sense of inner limitation you may be experiencing in your life. As you work with the suggestions throughout this book, your understanding of this new process will deepen and you'll find yourself spontaneously practicing this process in life—noticing more possibilities and seeing alternatives. You will feel more flexible, more open, and much more capable of handling whatever life dishes out to you.

Holistic Releasing™ is based on the premise that everything we experience in life, whether real or imagined, arises in pairs or polarities or duality. Because of life's underlying unity, if we have "in," we also have "out." If we have "right," we also have "wrong." If we have "good," we also have "bad." If we have "pain," we also have pleasure." This is quite obvious. However when we live life as though we can hold onto the good and get rid of the bad, we miss the inner truth. When we try to hold onto something good, it always slips away. Whenever we try to clutch onto what we judge as good or preferable, it tends to move through our awareness.

Then think about the converse. What happens when we resist or try to hold away what we don't like? That is right. It persists or gets even bigger. So in effect what we've been doing is pulling what we don't like towards us and pushing what we do like away. We also spend a lot of time and energy magnifying the polarity by trying to keep what we like as far away as possible from what we don't like. All of this is creating the exact opposite effect of what we want: magnifying or even creating what we call problems.

I have discovered that when you bring the two sides of a

polarity together, it's like bringing matter and antimatter together, or positive and negative energy. The pair neutralizes each other and you're left with much greater freedom, greater presence, and greater understanding. You see solutions, not problems. You feel more open, more alive, and more at peace. As you work with the material in this book, you'll discover that this effect magnifies over time. You will start to discover more possibilities and see things more clearly. Every time you work with any of the suggestions in this book, you'll get more out of them—more inner understanding.

Now, the way we do this is very simple. We simply focus on both sides of the polarity by going back and forth. For instance, a very simple polarity has to do with happiness. Most of us are either feeling relatively happy or unhappy from moment to moment, and we see only one, not the other. So let's just do a little experiment. Could you allow yourself to feel as unhappy as you do in this moment? And then, could you allow yourself to feel as happy as you do in this moment? And as unhappy as you do in this moment? And as happy as you do in this moment? Do this a few more times and then notice how you feel inside.

To practice Holistic Releasing™, I suggest you continually go back and forth on each side of the particular polarity you are exploring. Do this several times in a row and you'll notice something happening inside. The polarities dissolve each other. You may have already noticed this just by doing the exercise. You are left with greater and greater freedom and presence. You may see the underlying unity beneath the apparent duality and separation of the polarities. You may also experience it as an energetic shift. You may feel it as a sense of dissolving or clearing or lightness. You may have greater clarity and understanding within your own self.

The way to get the most out of this process is merely to stay as open and as fully engaged as you can from moment to moment. As you ask the questions or repeat the statements to yourself, please do so with as open a mind and a heart as possible, doing your best not to lead with either one. If you must lead with one, do your best to lead with your heart–your feeling sense. Allow yourself to be as open as you can to the thoughts, feelings, sensations, and pictures that arise when you repeatedly ponder the statements or questions. Even better, try not to do anything except to stay open on every level. Let this process–releasing–do you.

The initial results from working with a polarity may be subtle. But as you work with it, the results will become more and more profound. And if you're persistent in working on any particular polarity, you'll reach a place of neutrality, or you'll reach a place of great expansion inside, as you've dissolved your sense of limitation.

You may reach a point where you feel as though you've had enough. If this does happen, you can either allow yourself to relax even more into the process or simply take a break. Do something to break the pattern of the moment. Go for a walk, stand up and stretch, open your eyes and look around the room, or close your eyes if you had them open. Then come back to working with yourself.

Do your best to start noticing how you create artificial polarities in life and begin to bring the two sides of these polarities together. Even in noticing them they will start to dissolve, leaving you with growing understanding and freedom. Please let yourself enjoy this work that we do together. Allow it to be fun and easy. Remember, growth can be fun!

The following questions and answers will help you get the

most from the process of releasing. In addition to reading them now, review them as often as needed as you work through the material in this book.

How can I best do this process?

This process will help you to free yourself from all of your unwanted patterns of behavior, thought, and feeling. All that it requires from you is to be as open as you can to the process. It will free you to access clearer thinking, yet it is not a thinking process. It will help you to access heightened creativity, although you don't need to be particularly creative to be effective at doing this.

Sometimes we will use statements and sometimes we will use questions. When we use questions, we are merely asking you if it is possible to take this action. "Yes" or "No" are both acceptable answers. You will often let go even if you say, "No." As best you can, answer the question that you choose with a minimum of thought, staying away from second-guessing or getting into a debate with yourself about the merits of this action or its consequences. All the questions used in this process are deliberately simple. They are not important in and of themselves, but rather are designed to point you to the experience of letting go.

This process actually does itself. By simply switching back and forth in your mind between the two unique points of view that make up each polarity, they dissolve each other. As you work with this material, simply be as engaged as you can with an open mind and heart. Allow whatever thoughts, feelings, and limiting beliefs or pictures arise in your consciousness to just be there–welcome them as fully as you can. You do not even need to try and let them go. They will naturally dissolve each other.

What are some of the ways I can apply this in my life?

Any time you find yourself being able to perceive only one possibility, either internally or externally, there is a high likelihood that you are missing at least one or more possibilities. Develop the habit of looking for alternatives and then doing the releasing process to gain more inner clarity.

If you find yourself judging yourself or others, you can simply allow yourself to switch back and forth between the judgment you have and its opposite. If you find yourself stuck in any way, allow yourself to be as stuck as you are and as unstuck as you are. Allow yourself to be creative as you work with this process, and you will find yourself seeing more and more possibilities and opening to having it all including the ultimate happiness.

The following is a list of generic questions that you can use to work on your own issues and polarities:

Could I allow myself to resist _____ as much as I do?
Could I allow myself to welcome (allow) _____ as best as I can?

Could I allow myself to reject _____ as much as I do?
Could I allow myself to accept _____ as best as I can?

Could I allow myself to dislike _____ as much as I do?
Could I allow myself to like _____ as much as I do?

Could I allow myself to hate _____ as much as I do?
Could I allow myself to love _____ as best as I can?

Could I allow myself to want to change _____ as much as I do?
Could I allow myself to let go of wanting to change _____ as best I can?

Could I allow myself to say no to _____ ?

Could I allow myself to say yes to _____ ?

Could I allow myself to be as open to _____ as I am?
Could I allow myself to be as closed to _____ as I am?

What does it feel like to release?

The experience of releasing can widely vary depending on the individual. Most people feel an immediate sense of lightness or relaxation as they use the process. Others feel energy moving in their bodies as though they are coming back to life. You will also notice that your mind gets progressively quieter and your remaining thoughts clearer. You will start to see more solutions rather than just problems. Over time it may even feel positively blissful. The changes become more pronounced the longer you practice.

How do I know I'm doing it right?

If you notice any positive shifts in feeling, attitude, or behavior, then you are doing it right. However, every issue you work on may require different amounts of releasing. If at first it doesn't shift completely, release and release again. Continue releasing until you have achieved your desired result.

What if I feel I don't know how to release?

We were all born with the innate ability to let go. If you have ever watched a happy baby you know what I mean. Because this ability was not under our conscious control, over time we forgot how to do it. However, it is so natural that it doesn't require thinking, just as we don't think, "breathe," every time we take a breath.

Another way to look at it is with the example of a light

switch. The first time you turned a light switch did you know how it worked? Probably not. Nevertheless, the light turned on and you were able to experience the benefit of the light right away, before you ever understood how it operated.

The more you can lead with your heart and not your mind in this process, the easier it is to do. If you find you are getting stuck in wanting to figure it out, try letting go of the wanting to figure it out, and see what happens.

How could something this simple be so powerful?

The most powerful and usable things in life are often the simplest. When things are allowed to remain simple, they are easy to remember and duplicate.

No one has to convince you how critically important breathing is, yet if I were to give you a procedure to follow for breathing it would be: "Breathe in–breathe out. Repeat as needed." What could be simpler? Yet there is little that is more fundamental to your life. As you use Holistic Releasing™ over time, you will discover that it can become as easy as second nature and require as little thought as breathing does now.

What should I do if I find myself getting caught up into old patterns of behavior or I just plain forget to release?

First, it is important to remember that this is to be expected and it's OK. Your ability to release will increase over time. When you recognize that there is a problem, you can always release now.

When learning to release, you may go through the following progression:

1. You will do things just the way you did them before and you

will only remember to release afterwards. The moment you recognize that there is a problem, simply release.

2. Over time, you will start to catch yourself in the middle, when you are involved in the old behavior pattern. You can release when you recognize that you are doing it again, and you will find that you are able to change the old pattern.

3. Over more time, you will catch yourself about to get caught up in the pattern again and you will release and not do it.

4. Finally, you won't even need to release about that particular tendency because you will have completely let it go.

If you allow yourself to be persistent, your attitude and effectiveness will eventually change for the better, even about long-standing problems. It is also helpful to schedule short releasing breaks throughout your day to remind yourself to release.

Relax, Have Fun, and Enjoy

As you work through the book, you may find your life getting lighter and freer and more alive. You may also find that you start to uncover some of the universal truths for which you have been striving. Congratulations on beginning this journey to the place that you have never left–the heart of awareness. It is my sincerest hope that this material will quickly help you to discover and live a life filled with a happiness without sorrow, a joy without bounds, and a peace and bliss that surpass all understanding.

"If we could only be, just be,

we could see our infinity.

We could see that we are the all."

Lester Levenson

Session I

The Basic Goal and Ways to Attainment

That which every one of us is looking for in this world is exactly the same thing. Every Being, even the animal, is looking for it. And what is it that we are all looking for? Happiness with no sorrow! A continuous state of happiness with no taint whatsoever of sorrow. Now, if this is the goal, why is it the goal? The reason why it is the goal is because imperturbable happiness is our very basic nature! And what is imperturbable happiness? Complete and total freedom—and that is freedom to do or not to do anything and everything. This is the real natural state, before we encumber it with limitations.

Why is it that most of us do not have this continuous happiness with no sorrow? There is only one reason: being this infinite Being, we have done away with this happiness by thinking, "I am an individual, separate from the All," and thereby we have assumed limitation. To make myself separate from the All, I must set up a means to accomplish this. The means is my mind, and, with my mind, I create my body and the external world. Then I proceed, looking for the All in the external world, creating more and more thoughts and matter until the thoughts and matter have me so involved that I have forgotten my real identity as the infinite Beingness that I am.

The original thought of, "I am separate from the All" necessarily creates a feeling of lack and loneliness. I am only satisfied when I am the All. Seeking fulfillment of desire in the world therefore cannot undo the lack, as lack is not there in the first place; lack is assumed in my mind. Our totality is in our Beingness only, and we go on and on trying to satisfy desire externally, and we never, never succeed. If we could succeed, we would be able to satisfy desire, and, therefore, all desire would disappear!

The real purpose of being here on this earth is to learn, or to re-remember, our original natural state of totality of Beingness, which allows imperturbability with complete freedom and no limitation. Once we are led to see that this is our natural state, then we begin to let go of all the limitations.

The prime, the very first, limitation is the feeling, "I am an individual separate from the All." Eliminate that and you eliminate all loneliness, all limitation.

To say this in another way, "God is all! Let go and let God be. It is not I but the Father who worketh through me." We must let go of the ego sense, which is the original sense of our separation–from the All–and allow our natural Being to just be, and then everything will fall perfectly into line. However, even after this idea is accepted, we do not find it easy to accomplish. We don't find it easy because of habits that have been established since the beginning of time. And, for some reason, we like these habits, and so we continue them. We call them subconsciously-directed behavior, and we go on and on and on behaving automatically, as though we are a victim of our subconscious mind.

Now, the subconscious mind is only that part of the mind that we refuse to look at. When our desire for freedom is strong enough, we will dig up these subconscious habits, look at them and begin to let go of them.

There is no growing into the natural Being that you are. That Being is whole and perfect, here and now. There is only letting go of the concepts to the contrary—that you have limitations, that you have troubles. Anyone who says, "I have trouble," has it in his mind. That is the only place where it is, because you can't see or conceive of anything anywhere else but in your mind. Whatever you look at, whatever you hear, whatever you sense, is in and through your mind. That is where everything is. Change your think-ingness and you change your world for you. Do this and you have the proof!

So, the way to freedom—the path—is simple, but the method of undoing the limitations is not easy because of habit. We need a very strong desire to begin to let go of these habits. Without that strong desire, there is no growth. This desire must be stronger than the desire for the world—to control the external world or to have its approval.

The world as you now see it is really an imagination. When you see the truth, the world turns out to be a dream, a fiction in your mind. First you will see it as a dream, and then you will see it as a dream that never really was. It is exactly as what happens with a night dream. While you are in the night dream, you have a body. There are other bodies, there is action, interaction, there is good and there is bad. And so long as you remain in that night dream, everything there is real to you. When you awaken from the night dream, you say, "My gosh, it was just a dream! It never really happened! This dream was all in my mind!" And in exactly the same manner you will awaken from this dream called the waking state. You come to see that it was only a fiction of your imagination; it was only a dream. And then you let go of it–lock, stock and barrel, and what is left over is the infinite you! Then you are called fully realized, totally free.

Actually, we are fully realized all the time. We are fully realized Beings saying that we are not. So, all we do is let go of "we are not," and what is left over is the fully realized and free Being that we are.

Are there any questions on what I've said so far? No? Then everyone understands this, at least intellectually.

All right, if you understand this intellectually, and you are not able to use it, it is because you are not looking at yourself honestly, truthfully, with a deep desire to let go of your limitations. You have set up in your subconscious mind all the things you will not look at, and they have culminated as inhibiting and compulsive feelings. It is necessary that you release all the inhibiting and compulsive feelings. You are now run by them, you are a victim of them. By releasing them, your mind quiets, and you become free. Therefore, undo these limiting feelings and thoughts, quiet the mind and this infinite Being that you are becomes self-obvious. Then you see that you never were subjected to that mind, that body, and from that moment on, the mind and body have no influence upon you. You then determine for the body as you would a puppet, and it has no more effect upon you than a puppet would.

So, the very best method of all methods is to quiet the mind by releasing all subconscious feelings and thoughts, and there remains the Being that you are.

"What am I?" is the final question that everyone answers, so why not begin with the final question? If you can, all good, all wonderful. But there are very few of us who are capable of using this method of just holding onto "What am I?" We have gotten ourselves so habituated with subconscious thoughts and feelings that we cannot let go of them; therefore, we need other methods, other aids. The other major methods from the East are called Jnana Yoga, Raja or Kriya Yoga, Bhakti Yoga and Karma Yoga. The path that is best for you is the one that you like best.

Each path includes all the other paths. The only difference is the emphasis. If we are intellectual, we emphasize the Jnana path, the path of intellect and wisdom. If we are of devotional nature, we emphasize the Bhakti path of love and devotion to God. If we like to be of service to mankind, we use the Karma Yoga path. Each path leads to the quieting of the mind, enough so that we may see the infinite Being that we are.

Since all the above paths aim to achieve the quieting of the mind, why not go directly to the mind itself? That would be direct and practical and the most efficient of methods. If we examine the mind, we will discover that it is simply the totality of all our thoughts, conscious and subconscious, and that all our past thoughts on particular things have culminated in feelings. The feeling now motivates the thoughts. If our thoughts are motivated by our feelings, all we need to do is release our feelings, the motivators of the thoughts. Then our mind will be quiet. When the mind is quieted, the infinite Being that we are is what is left over and is self-obvious. Simple, is it not?

Following the above, there fell into place a simple method that anyone can understand and use. It is called the Sedona Method®, and information about it is available to anyone who will write for it.

Let us now take a look at this so-called apparency: the world. The world is only an imagination that we created mentally. It is not external, but in reality is within us, within our mind. Someday you will discover that you created the entire universe that you see. Creation began by first creating what we call a mind. The mind then imagined the world. Thus we created our mind, which is a composite of all our thoughts and feelings, conscious and subconscious, and in which is our world.

Every little thing that happens to each and every one of us is created in our thinking. We mentally set up a thing called time that makes it even more difficult to see the creation process, because we think now and the effect of that thought happens much later. But the only creator there is is mind, your mind. Is God a creator? Yes, because you are. Thou are That! You set up a mind and, through the mind, create.

It is necessary and good to discover that everything happening to us is caused by our feeling and thinking. Everything that happens to us is created first in our thought. When you discover that you created your trouble, then you realize that you can create anything you desire and will create only good things.

After you discover that there is nothing that you cannot create, you are still not satisfied. The reason is that you have separated yourself from your infinite Beingness, your Oneness, and only upon recognizing and being your infinite Beingness are you perfectly satisfied. So if there are any problems that remain, they only remain because you are holding onto them in your thought. The moment you let go of them, they are gone! If you tell me that isn't so for you, that isn't true. The truth is you are still holding onto them, telling me that it doesn't work. Trying to get rid of a problem is holding onto it. Anything we try to get rid of, we are holding in mind and thereby sustaining it. So, the only way to correct a problem is to let go of it. See not the problem, see only what you want. If you would only from this moment on see what you want, that is all that you would get. But you hold in mind the things you do not want. You struggle to eliminate the things you don't want, thereby sustaining them. So, it is necessary to let go of the negative and put in the positive if you want a positive, happy life.

This subject cannot be learned intellectually; it cannot be learned in the mind, because truth is perceived just behind the mind. We can use the mind to release the mind so that by getting it quieter we can see behind the mind. If it were possible to get this subject through the mind intellectually, all we would need to do is to read the books on it and we would have it. But it doesn't work that way. We have to concentrate in order to seek our Self that is just behind the mind. Turn the mind back upon the mind to release the mind, and then you may go beyond the mind to your Self. To understand, each one must experience it, realize it, make it real by going to the place just behind the mind and perceiving it there, and then you know and know that you know. Then you operate intuitively, from the realm of all-knowingness.

Now, the very highest state is simply Beingness, and if we could only be, just be, we could see our Infinity. We would see that we are the All. We would be in a perfectly satiated, permanent, changeless state. And this state is not a nothingness, it is not a boredom, it is an Allness, an Everythingness, a total satiation that is eternal. You will never, never lose your individuality. The feeling "I" as you use it to mean your individuality will never, ever leave you. It expands. What happens as you discover what you are is that you begin to see that others are you, that you are me, that there is only One, that you are now and always have been that one and glorious Infinite Being.

Comments:

You are already unlimited Beingness. You are already the happiness that you are seeking in everything else you do. You are now and have always been, and every path or technique is designed only to make you, as Lester often put it, "self obvious to yourself." Lester also often asked: "How long should it take for an unlimited being to discover their unlimitedness?" It does not need to take any time whatsoever, since you already are what you are seeking. Please rest in this knowingness as best you can as work through this course.

Suggestions for the week:

If happiness without sorrow is a goal that you would like to pursue, the following exercise will help you to start to discover the unlimited happiness that you already are.

Make a list of persons, places, things, and accomplishments or situations that you believe will make you happy, and allow yourself to explore these in the following ways.

With each item on your list ask yourself: "Could I let go of wanting to get happiness from (your item) and allow myself to rest as the happiness that I already am?"

You do not have to believe you are happiness to get value from this exercise. Just allow yourself to remain open to the possibility. Also, as you work down your list, remember that there is nothing wrong with having most of what you will write. We are not saying you should not have these things. We are merely suggesting that it is possible to have and be happiness whether or not you have them.

As you discover this, you will bring your natural state of happiness more and more to everything that you have, be, or do.

You can also work with each item using this polarity: My happiness comes from (your item)–I am the happiness that I am seeking.

With both of these techniques of working on happiness, you can also do them throughout your day when you notice yourself postponing happiness to some future time, even if that is something small like having lunch or going out on a date or winning an unimportant point in an argument. We are postponing happiness most of the time without even being aware of it. As you let go of postponing happiness in these ways, you will discover a deepening sense of happiness that will be with you all the time enhancing all the things that you used to think you required in order to be happy.

Throughout the week you may also want to explore this polarity: I am an individual separate from the All–I am the All.

As you work with this polarity, allow yourself to explore the possibility that all separation is an illusion that we made up in order to have a false sense of security.

The next seven pages of this book are designed to help further your own exploration. You can view them as your diary of progress during the week that you are working with this session. Use the space allowed on each page to write down your gains and realizations as they happen, as well as for notes on working with the various exercises.

Day One

Day Two

Day Three

Day Four

Day Five

Day Six

Day Seven

"If we don't like what's happening to us

in the world, all we have to do

is change our consciousness—

and the world out there changes for us!"

Lester Levenson

Session 2

Problems and How They Resolve

Do you want me to talk, or do you want to ask questions? I guess I could start with telling you my impressions of what has happened to you since I was here last year.

We seem to have greater, more intense problems. This is for all in general, not anyone in particular. This intensification of problems makes it appear as though we are going backwards, but it isn't true. We have risen to the state where we can better express ourselves outwardly. We are expressing our problems out in the world more rather than holding them dormant in the subconscious mind. When we are apathetic, it's difficult for us to express, and it's difficult for us outwardly to act. So our problems remain unresolved, swirling around in our subconscious mind. They don't come out and materialize in the world and make a solution possible.

When we begin to move a step above the apathetic state, we begin to acquire more capability of action in the world. Then our problems manifest outwardly in the world, and it seems as though the world is falling in on us. But it's actually a state of growth to move up from the apathetic state into the beginnings of the doing-ness state. This is the state of apathetic-doingness. When we come into this apathetic-doingness state, we begin to do—with apathetic, agitated tendencies—and therefore we're somewhat destructive, even to ourselves. We become outwardly or expressively destructive to the world and to ourselves; we seem to have more problems and things seem worse. We think we're going backwards, but we're actually moving ahead, because apathetic-doingness is higher than apathetic non-doingness.

Now, the step above apathetic-doingness is one of doingness in which we are equally constructive and destructive. Move up another step and we move into the doingness-beingness state where we're big doers and where we are only constructive. When we step up from there, we go into the beingness state: we don't have to do, we only just be, we only just are.

The world today is in a state of apathetic-doingness. It has moved up into this state and therefore has bigger problems. Although this appears otherwise, it is progress, a step forward from stage 1 to stage 2.

The foregoing stages of growth are set out in the chart on the next page.

Stages of Growth

INACTION

1. Apathy: Inaction, due to apathy, with resentments, hostilities and fear to express for fear of retaliation. A subjectively destructive state.

2. Apathetic-doingness: Beginnings of action, having enough will to express outwardly. A beginning of an outwardly active but destructive state.

ACTION

3. Doingness: Action that moves us out of Stage 1 toward the equilibrium of Stage 5. Here one is equally constructive and destructive to oneself and to the world.

4. Doingness-beingness: Energetic doingness with calmness; much outward action, all constructive to oneself, the world and the universe.

INACTION - INNER ACTION

5. Beingness: Inaction due to serenity; the ability to just be; witnessing, watching, allowing and accepting the world and universe as it is.

Q: Is this the world in general, or is it just the people on the path who are caught up in this?

Lester: It's both. We are all involved in this. You see it expressed in the race issue, the revolt against the establishment, juvenile delinquency, Vietnam, Africa. It's prevalent everywhere today. It is part of the world growth (Stage 2).

Q: Is this because people are more developed to cope with the world?

Lester: They're more developed, not to cope with the worldly problems but to do something about them. The way they're trying to cope with them is a destructive way. Problems could be solved by discussions, and should be. However, the state the world is in, one of apathetic-doingness, is a step forward from the lower state of pure apathy with no doingness. The world today is in a slow state of Beingness (Stage 2). It's a materialistic age.

About 1700 AD, we came out of the lowest state, a period of physical, animal sensuality wherein we lived only to satiate our appetites. You know what the Dark Ages were. We're now in the second period wherein we can enjoy the finer, more cultural things, and we're still having the growing pains of getting out of the first into the second. But the second is not a highly spiritual state. It's the period where, in the world, we advance scientifically. The third period begins the era of knowing that this is a mental world and that we are all related. We are more loving to one another and we stop fighting each other. The fourth period is the state in which man knows fully his Beingness in God, that his and everyone's Beingness is God. He knows he is a free, unlimited being.

These four periods are the Iron, Bronze, Silver and Golden Ages the ancient Greeks spoke of. (The fifth stage is really beyond this world although it is accomplished in this world.) However, at any time, whenever anyone chooses, they may move into the highest state. We don't have to stay at the level that the world is in, and those of us who are on the path are moving up out of this general level. Aren't we lucky?

Q: Even with our problems?

Lester: Yes. To people in the world, everything seems hopeless. They feel helpless, but we know the way out. No matter how much the world hurts us, we know there's a way out. We have hope and a direction.

And what is the way out? Not looking to the world for happiness, but looking to the place where happiness is, right within us, within our own consciousness. Unlimited joy is our natural, inherent state. We have, through ignorance, undone it by imposing concepts of limitations: I need this, I need him, I need her, and if I don't get what I want, I am hurt, I have trouble. Growth is only letting go of these concepts of lack and limitation, or, on the positive side, going within and seeing this unlimited Being that we are.

Any time we have trouble, any time we have a problem, we are being the limited ego. We are trying to express the Self through the limited ego, and it's too small; we get squeezed, and it hurts. So, if there is a problem, the thing to do is to ask yourself, "What am I doing? Wherein am I demanding with ego motivation?" If the answer comes, if you see how, ego-wise, you're causing this so-called problem, you will pull the causative thought up from the subconscious into the conscious. Once it is conscious, you will naturally let go of it.

If you don't let go of it, the reason why is that the cause, the thought that initiated the difficulty, remains subconscious. So, either we make the thought conscious and let go of it, or—and this is the higher and the better way—we know strongly enough that we are the Self. Knowing that we are the perfect Self, that we are not this limited body and mind, all problems immediately resolve. It sounds quite indicting when I say any problem, any trouble, is ego motivated, but that, you'll find, is true. When you be just your Self, there is no problem, there is nothing that does not fall into line perfectly, harmoniously, with no effort. The more ego motivated you are, the more difficult it is to accomplish something, the less is the harmony and the greater is the misery. It is really as simple as I'm putting it.

What is not easy is to let go of the wrong habit of insisting upon being an ego. This habit is strong. It has been deeply ingrained over thousands of years. We are now letting go of it, but we don't let go of it easily because the habit has been there for such a long, long time. However, the moment we choose to let go of it, we can. If we say we can't let go, it's because we really don't want to. The desire to let go isn't strong enough.

Do I make this too simple? You know why I'm addressing you, because I know you've had quite a lot of this. You have probably heard it presented in complicated ways, with a lot of things added to it that make it more difficult to see. But once we accept it and see the simplicity of it, all we need to do is effect it. And no one can do it for us. We have to do it ourselves.

Q: I have a friend who has problems. She's Catholic and very pious. When things get blackest and she has no more hope and is at the bottom, at that very moment, something happens so that everything turns out right.

Lester: Do you know why she must reach bottom?

Q: Well, she has faith and she knows that—

Lester: No, she doesn't have faith, and she is not pious. This is her trouble. You see, faith would cause her to let go and let God—being pious, being humble and surrendering, would cause the same thing. Outwardly, she's the way you say, but inwardly she's the way I'm saying. You see, she tries herself to control everything, and that's not letting go and letting God.

Q: She prays.

Lester: Yes, she prays, but she wants it the way she wants it. She's found out that her praying for it doesn't help her. If you surrender, you don't have to pray. You've got to let go and let God. When does she let go and let God? When she herself can't do anything anymore, she lets go. In the extreme, she lets go—and the moment one lets go, everything resolves itself. Can you see that? When things reach the extreme, she feels, "Oh, there's nothing I can do," and that's when she lets go and lets God. If you can show her this point, she'll see it, most likely, and then be more consciously able to use it.

Q: I keep trying to tell her that she must be confident.

Lester: Conviction, which is stronger than faith–absolute conviction of God–that will do it! Let go and let God and then everything straightens out. But when we try to do it, we have trouble.

Q: When you say, "Let go and let God," does that mean that you should work strictly on inspiration, or should you just sit back and let things happen?

Lester: Have the feeling of "letting things happen." To accomplish this, we have to let the ego-sense go. The ego is the feeling, "I am an individual, Lester, and I have a body and I do things." That's wrong. I have to get Lester out of the way and let God or Self operate. When this is achieved, you'll sort of float through things, and there will be no effort. If there is effort, there is ego.

Of course, now you're going to have to use some effort, because you're not starting off as the realized Self. You see, only when this girl goes to the extreme does she let go of the sense of doership and then things happen effortlessly. That's letting go and letting God!

Professing faith, professing all these things, doesn't do it–actually having them does it. The fact that she has troubles is proof that she doesn't have the conviction of God, because God is All. God is Perfect, and if God is All and God is Perfect, everything must be perfect and that leaves no place for imperfection or troubles. If you take that attitude, so be it! It is the feeling that I am not the doer, and that I let go and let it happen.

Q: I can't tell when I'm ego.

Lester: When there's no effort, there's no ego. The more the effort the more the ego.

Q: When the effort is extreme, you have to more or less go the other way, anyway.

Lester: Yes. I'm trying to give you a method of knowing whether it's ego or not. The more the effort the greater the ego. However, you're going to use effort until you're fully realized. Now, there will be times when you'll use no effort, and everything will fall perfectly into line for you. At these times, you'll be your Self.

Q: But doesn't this type of thing make you indolent, so that you don't do any action? Is it that you shouldn't try to do anything? That's what I don't understand.

Lester: Indolence is an action, a negative action. It is the act of holding yourself from moving. It is impossible now for you to be actionless. To achieve the actionless state, you should try to let go of your ego more and more, because now you can't do it totally. If you could, you'd be fully realized. But if you keep letting go of the ego, you will eventually drop it and then be the witness rather than the doer. Does that make sense? Be not the doer. Let it happen. Have the feeling, It's God's world, whatever is happening, so let Him!

Q: How do we get rid of problems?

Lester: The moment you say, "I have a problem," you are stuck—you are making it real! You can't get rid of the problem, because you are making it real. You've got it.

Q: So, if when we have problems, we say, "There is no problem at all," will they vanish then?

Lester: No. If you say, "There is no problem," they won't vanish, because you're saying, "There is no problem." You're mentally holding the problem in mind and therefore sustaining it. Erase the problem from your mind. Know that everything is perfect–then the problem is necessarily nonexistent.

Q: I think that way, that everything is really perfect.

Lester: If you really do, then everything must be.

Q: How easy it would be if we understood this from the beginning.

Lester: Yes. You see, naturally, life should be totally effortless. There is no effort in life whatsoever when we are just being our natural Self. But we're trying to be a limited ego–that takes effort. It takes effort to be limited when your natural state is unlimited. The more you try to be limited, the more effort it takes.

To be your unlimited Self takes no effort. Just like your friend: when she gets to the extreme, she lets go and everything straightens out, with no effort. All the time she tries and tries, things get worse and worse. But when she gives up and lets go, things resolve.

Q: Well, she had to go out and look for a job. She had to go to an agent, she just couldn't sit down and wait.

Lester: I say all she had to do was to let go and let God. Then, even if she had locked herself in a chamber somewhere, the things would have come to her. You don't sit down and wait, you don't do anything. Just let go of the sense of doership. You just know that everything is perfect, and then the slightest thought you have will come into being quickly. There's no limitation on God, the Self. Whatever you think will have to come into being if you let go, because you're invoking your infinite power—God, your Self. Nothing can stop it!

Q: But at the same time you have to struggle to get some action.

Lester: No, I said just the opposite. I said lock yourself in a chamber and padlock it, and if you will do what I'm saying, you'll find that what you want will be effected. It has to be. Nothing can stop it! Omnipotence is invoked!

Q: What is prayer for? What does praying mean?

Lester: Praying is for those who need praying. When you know what you know, to whom are you praying? If you are That, why do you have to pray to It? Praying admits duality: "I" pray to "God." Maintain your Oneness!

However, when one does pray, it is best to pray for one thing only: more wisdom so that you eliminate all need for any prayer, for any asking. It all depends on one's state of understanding. Most people in the world today need to pray. But prayer admits duality—God is "out there." And we should know that God is within. Even though Jesus said, "The kingdom of God is within," we still look for God without, and He's not out there. He's only within. He turns out to be our very own Beingness.

The "I" of us, with nothing added to it, is the God we seek. When you say, "I am something," that isn't It, or, "I and something," that too isn't God. But just pure "I" and only "I," that is God. That is why it is said that God is closer than flesh. It is "I," and how close is "I"? It's closer than flesh. It is God, your very own Self!

Q: That's a very good feeling.

Lester: Yes, because it's reminding you of what you know subconsciously, that you are that Self. Just hold on to the word "I" only, "I, I, I, I," and you'll become more exhilarated. Try it when you're alone. Just "I, I, I," and not, "I am a body, I am a mind," but, "I, I, I," that feeling of Being. I think the word that describes God better than any other single word is "Beingness." God is all Beingness. We are all Beingness pretending we're a tiny part of It, a limited body-mind. When you look within, you'll see that you are all Beingness. Beingness is God! Beingness is also awareness, consciousness. They are the same thing. Later on, you'll see them as identical, Beingness and consciousness. So, be your Self, and there never will be a problem.

Seeing a problem in the world is trying to be a limited ego-body-mind. If you think you have a problem, you do. If you'll just accept that God is All, God is perfect, that that's all there is and look at perfection, then that's all you'll ever meet with!

Q: Then we have to wipe out the word "problem."

Lester: Yes. You have to wipe out the words "problem," "can't," "don't," "won't" —all negative words. In the future, when man is in a state of harmony, all these words will disappear.

Q: As you progress more on the path, so many things seem so much more superficial. I don't know if that's progress, or if I'm becoming indifferent to the world around me.

Lester: Well, that is progress—being indifferent, that is, non-attached.

Q: I really couldn't care less about politics or all these things that at one time seemed so important. Is that bad?

Lester: How does it feel?

Q: I haven't analyzed the feeling. I've just seen that all these people think that what they're doing is so important. Maybe I'm wrong in that I don't feel that way.

Lester: No, you are right. The higher you go, the more you see the perfection, and therefore the less you see problems. The more one sees problems, the lower one is. What you're talking about is problems. The people who see them want you to see the way they see and will tell you that you're wrong. This is one thing you must be on guard against. As you grow, those who are not up to you will try to pull you down to where they are. Let them think you are wrong. You know you are right! Don't argue. It's fruitless.

Q: I find that people try to make me feel selfish because I feel that way. I don't know whether that's true or not. That is why I wanted to discuss it.

Lester: It's this way: When you don't think the way they think, they call you selfish. Just check it out. No, it's not how much you recognize a problem that shows unselfishness. It's how much you see that there is no problem and help others see that there is only perfection that shows unselfishness. This way you offer help; you're very constructive and unselfish.

Q: Just do everything with a desire to help, and that is love?

Lester: Yes. Just feel love—you don't necessarily have to do. Love and your thoughts are positive. Thought is far more powerful than action. It's the basis of and effects action. It is the initiator. It comes before and determines action. A realized being sitting in a cave somewhere all by himself is doing more good for the world than organizations of action. He is aiding everyone, as his help is being subconsciously received by all.

Now we're back to what we were talking about before: the bottom state is inaction, the middle state is action, and the top state is inaction. The bottom state is one of apathetic inertia. It's destructive. It just wants to stop everything, actually destroy everything.

The top state lets everything be just the way it is, because everything is perfect, and one in this state powerfully projects this mentally to everyone. The middle state is the action state that moves you from the bottom toward the top state of equilibrium and tranquility. As you move up, those who are not as far along as you are will try to pull you down to where they are.

Q: So, it's sort of a proving ground, or a testing, to see how much those things bother you.

Lester: Yes. It bests your conviction. Where is your conviction if you go with them? If you go with them your tendency is to believe more the way they do.

Q: Which is easier, I know.

Lester: No, try it. If you think it's easier, just go their way, and you'll have more misery, as they do.

Q: Sometimes it's easier just to be one of the mob.

Lester: Desire for ego approval makes it seem easier. You'll find out otherwise. You've been one of the mob, haven't you? You've been like them. It's not easy. No, the right way is easier. Do you see that? The right way is letting go and letting God and then everything falls into line perfectly–no effort. But when I have to do it, it's not God, it's me–the ego–wanting to do, to change things, correct this world and so forth.

Q: Would a mantra or something like that be the best thing to remember when these things come up that way?

Lester: Affirmations are always good. A mantra is an affirmation

ated again and again. Do whatever will help you to do
___ ~~ wnat you think you should do and be.

Q: That's what I don't know.

Lester: To seek who and what you are, to know your Self, is the very
best thing to do and be. There've been moments when you've let go
and felt your real Self. How does it feel?

Q: Marvelous! Could I have it all the time?

Lester: Yes, certainly. Stay that way, that's all. Be what you are!
You're infinite, omniscient, omnipotent, right here and now. Be
That! Stop being this limited, miserable, little ego.

Q: Well, I have the same problem he has, and I thought I was
becoming indifferent.

Lester: Yes, you're becoming indifferent to the negativity, and
what's wrong with that? What is politics? It's a mechanism of force
and control. In a society where everyone loves everyone, do you
need politics? If you want to help the world, help yourself grow, and
you'll do far more than you could by being involved in politics. The
more you're capable of loving, the more you're helping the world.
Parliaments cannot right the world, but enough people loving can.
The President of the United States must necessarily represent the
sum total consciousness, the sum total thinkingness, of all the people of the United States added together. The world out there is only
our collective consciousness. Principle, divine law supercedes

man-made law. Consciousness, thinkingness, determines every-thing. If we don't like what's happening to us in the world, all we have to do is change our consciousness and the world out there changes for us!

Q: But doesn't this sort of thing take a great deal of courage many times? Sometimes I don't really have the guts to be able to do the things I want to do.

Lester: All right, why don't you have the guts?

Q: I don't know.

Lester: Ego. You want approval from them. You're seeking their approval; you want to go the way they want you to go.

Q: It isn't that I want their approval, I don't want their disapproval.

Lester: Well, isn't that the same thing?

Q: I remember you said last time that when you resolve a problem, it doesn't come up again, and it's true. But then you get new ones. When you have solved something within your own mind, and you know that you have come up a step on the ladder, it doesn't pres-ent itself again, which is a great help, but then there are always new problems.

Lester: There's no end to problems in the world. You go on and on forever and ever solving problems in the world, and you'll have more and more. As long as you are conscious of problems, they exist. Only when you discover the real you are there no problems. What you do is put your hand in a fire and say, "Ouch, it's hot! My hand is burning! Boy, do I have a problem!" That's all.

When you see that you are doing it, you stop. If you have a problem, you're putting your hand into a problem and yelling, "It hurts!" and acting as though you're not putting your hand into it. You act as though you are not doing it, but you are. That problem is in your consciousness. It's in your mind. Change your mind, change your consciousness, and immediately that problem is no more. Try it and you'll see that it's so.

Q: Last year, when we were all meeting together, we were higher and we had fewer problems.

Lester: That's the prime purpose of coming together as a group. You're reminded and supported in your direction. You're with people who are striving in that same direction. You are moving opposite to the way the world is moving. You need positive company as much as possible. And when you are by yourself, stop being what you are not–a limited body and mind and just be what you are–an infinite, totally free, grand and glorious being, whole and complete.

Comments:

Look within yourself and see if you are willing to live in a world without problems. If there is any hesitancy, it is probably because, without realizing it, you want to create problems in your life. We do this because as long as we think we are a limited body-mind we feel like we need be like everyone else and to have a purpose in life. We are afraid if there were no problems there would be no need for us. And in a way we are right. Who we are not—our limited body-mind-ego—thrives on creating and then solving problems in order to justify its existence. The less we are invested in limitation, the less we need to create problems to resolve, and the less we even see problems in the world. As Lester repeatedly said, "See the perfection where the seeming imperfection seems to be."

Another way to look at this is: If God is the only doer and God is perfect, how can there be a problem? We only perceive problems when we feel like it is "me" who is doing, as opposed to resting in the knowing that, "It is not I but the father who worketh through me." The more you accept this without hold back, the less you will see problems even if everyone around you does. You will also have more of a positive effect on those around you because you are also holding the perfection for them and seeing them as their beingness as opposed to a limited body-mind.

Suggestions for the week:

This week, if you see problems in your life, ask yourself, "What frustrated ego desire is causing this problem?" If you allow yourself to be truly open to see yourself clearly you will see the ego desire and if it does not let go spontaneously simply ask yourself, "Could I let go of wanting that?"

Also, if you notice that at times you would rather fit in than be the beingness that you are, you can ask yourself: "Would I rather fit in or would I rather be free?" This will probably cause you to drop your wanting love and be stronger in your desire for freedom. If there is a hesitation, just ask yourself, "Could I let that go?" And just decide to drop this desire.

Here are some polarities you can also work on to support your understanding:

- There are problems–There are no problems
- There is a problem–Everything is perfect.
- This is my picture–This is God's picture.
- I am the doer–God is the only doer.

The next seven pages of this book are designed to help you further your own exploration. You can view them as your diary of progress during the week that you are working with this session. Use the space allowed on each page to write down your gains and realizations as they happen, as well as for notes on working with the various exercises.

Day One

Day Two

Day Three

Day Four

Day Five

Day Six

Day Seven

"The only growth there is,

is the elimination of the ego."

Lester Levenson

Session 3

Spiritual Growth

This session is composed of aphorisms compiled from various talks by Lester. Allow yourself to ponder them one at a time. Give yourself enough time to gain the maximum benefit that each has to offer before moving on to the next.

- The whole object on the path is to let go of the ego. What remains is your Self.

- The only growth there is is the eliminating of the ego.

- Ego is the sense that "I am an individual, separate from the All." In the extreme, it is egotism.

- Growth is transcending yourself, your habitual self, which is none other than ego.

- Growth is the ego getting out of its misery.

- Recognize that all joy is nothing but your Self, more or less.

- There is no happiness except that of experiencing your Self. When you see that, it makes the path very direct. You stop chasing the rainbow, and you go for the happiness where you know it is—right within you.

- Everything you are seeking you are and very foolishly saying you are not. That's part of the enigma: everything everyone is seeking with such intensity, one has—and much more.

- It is you. When you say, "I," that is the Infinite. Great big joke! Here you are, infinite and looking for your Self, which you are!

- When anyone says he is not a master, he is lying.

- Your effort should be for proper identity—identify with your Self!

- Spiritual advancement is determined by how much you identify with your real Self.

- The ego is very tricky. It often talks us out of this path for a short period of time, sometimes for a longer period of time. But once we've gotten into it, we usually almost always come back to it. So, you have to be careful of the trickery of the ego part of us. It can really take us away. No matter how far we have advanced on the path, the ego is always a treacherous companion that can take us off the path, sometimes for an entire lifetime.

- This is something we should be on guard against. The ego-sense latches on and says, "I am God." It latches onto the progress, and it feels good, and it says, "I am It." By doing so, it sabotages further growth.

- When you recognize the opposition of the ego, you can let go of it. After practice, it is easy; and after you let go of enough ego, you just naturally feel the peace and joy of your Self.

- It's actually a path of taking on more and more of your natural state of being infinite. You give up limitation. You give up misery, but you never give up anything worthwhile. You never give up anything good.

- On this path, you constantly give up trouble.

- The first teacher is misery. It is usually the first thing that causes us to seek the way out.

- First, we start on the path to escape misery, then we taste the Self and want It because It tastes so good.

- On the path, you never give up anything–you just take on more and more of what you really want until you have the All.

- Take it for the sweetness that's in it, not to get out of the bitterness that's out of it.

- We discover that we never give up anything on the spiritual path but our self-imposed bondages and miseries.

- If you are weakly for the path, you are strongly for the sense-world.

- You think you can't, that's why you can't. It's only the thought, "I can't do it" that stops you from doing it.

- Those who can't don't really want to.

- Your growth depends only on you.

- It will happen as fast as you can do it.

- The only one who is going to change you is you!

- Wishing won't do it, nor will trying. You have got to do it!

- Good intentions are no substitute for right action.

- To change more rapidly, expect it!

- You must have a very strong desire to change, because you are such a victim of habit that you want the world as much as a drowning man wants air. To offset that, you must want to know your Self as much as a drowning man wants air.

- Your success is determined by your desire for it. If you get discouraged, you are not really interested.

- Your only real friend is you. Your only real enemy is you. You are an enemy to yourself to the degree you limit your Self. You are a friend to yourself to the degree you remove limits from yourself.

- What you do to yourself, it being of your own doing, only you can undo. You did it, you must undo it.

- This entire path is a do-it-yourself path.

- Do what is available to you to do. Do your best.

- Every experience is to bless you, not to hurt you. If you stay in accord with principle, you will come out higher!

- Every place and every situation in life presents an opportunity for growth.

- The best place to grow is right where you are. The best time is now.

- Be thankful for the opportunities to grow.

- The greatest of all tests are those at home, with your immediate family. Therefore, home is an excellent place to grow.

- A lot of spiritual growth can be had by practicing the real, selfless love on your mate and family.

- It is a good opportunity to grow when people are saying things about you, opposing you. It gives you a chance to practice the real Love. It gives you a chance to practice the real peace. Just because they are making sounds with their mouths is no reason why you should feel bad about it. Opposition is a very healthy thing. It provokes and firms growth.

- It is necessary to remember that everyone can be our teacher. If we react to praise or pleasantries, that is developing ego. If we're depressed over criticism, that is ego. When we are our Self, there is no reacting.

- There isn't anything that happens that can't be used. There's no incident that cannot be used as a teacher.

- Every minute of every day should be used to grow by.

- If we assume that we are there and we are not, circumstances soon awaken us to the fact that we are not.

- If you tell others of your high experiences, of your gains, because of their jealousy, they might say, "Ah, who does she think she is?" And that works against you and tends to pull you down.

- Any time you brag about anything, you're inviting a test of it. So, I warn you, if you are growing into these things, when they start coming–unless you're so sure you know by experience you can't lose it–it's better not to tell anyone.

- Be proud of your spiritual accomplishments. Be happy with them. Be proud of them to yourself.

- When you have false spiritual pride, you invite a challenge of the thing that you are proud of, and it is necessary to do away with doubts.

- It takes more than faith. It takes knowledge. You start with faith, but you must convert it to knowledge. You must test it out, and then you know it.

- In order to really understand, we must experience the knowledge.

- When you experience, it is no longer intellectual.

- You can get understanding without being able to put it into words.

- The only maturity there is, is spiritual understanding.

- Stand ye out and be different, and don't let the others trick you back into where you were. It's not easy. It takes fortitude.

- We should try to go all the way. To us, it is given to do that. We have the possibility of going all the way back home, right to the Absolute.

- Expect infinity, no more. You cannot expect too much.

- Toe the line to the very end. The more you toe the line, the sooner the end.

- Every gain is an eternal gain; every step forward you make now is forever.

- We climb a ladder, and each time we get up to another rung, we forget about the rungs below. Then, when we get to the top, we kick the ladder away.

- The proof of this subject is the result you get.

- The more you grow, the less you feel the need to grow.

- The higher you go, the less the incentive to go further.

- You never learn anything by disproving; you learn only by proving.

- Studying the illusion helps make it real. If you want to know the truth, don't study the opposite.

- The whole process of growth is letting go of thoughts. When our thoughts are totally eliminated, there is nothing left but the Self.

- Don't try to complicate it—it's too simple.

- We can only expand out of the ego. The Self is.

- Growth is letting go of being what you are not.

- Let go of your ego and be your Self!

- As you grow, the whole world opens wide for you—you experience so much more. However, even if you have this whole world, you've only got a dot. Take the whole cosmos!

- Longing for liberation is the key. Once you get that, you'll be carried all the way.

- In our desire to attain liberation or realization, we are helped to the degree that we help all others.

- Grow to the point where your whole attention is off you and on others.

- Why shouldn't we all be masters, all of us, here and now?

- The moment we decide to be the Self—really decide—it is so!

- The higher you go, the more non-difference comes. You accept the leaders of all religions alike.

- Having peace under ideal conditions isn't indicative of spiritual growth, it is escape.

- When people are not growing, they are going in the opposite direction.

- You should thank those who oppose you, because they give you an unusual opportunity for growth.

- When we start concerning ourselves with what they are doing, we're turning away from what we are doing.

- You need constant confirmation until you don't need it anymore.

- Perseverance is necessary.

- Adversity is a prod to growth.

- The more intense the crises in this world, the more we have an opportunity to grow.

- It would be so fast if people would, with constant, intense effort ask, "What am I?"

- When you get that answer, then you have control over your body and mind.

- If there is anything you don't like out there, there is a need to change yourself.

- You may see fully who you are and not be able to maintain it. What happens is that, being the infinite Self, we can get a glimpse of the infinite, hold it for a while, and then suddenly feel as though we've lost it. The reason for that is that the mind has not been eliminated. The subconscious thoughts of limitation are submerged for the moment. You may go completely into your Self and let go of the mind temporarily. You haven't eliminated the mind, you just momentarily let go of it.

  So there you are, for the moment, totally the infinite Self. However, the mind that has been submerged reemerges, and then the ego takes over, and you just can't understand what happened to you, what brought you back into the heaviness of the world again. What is required is that we re-establish that state of the Self again and again until it becomes permanent. Each time we do it, we scorch more of the mind, until finally we have scorched the entire mind. Then we are permanently established in the Self. Then you sit back, and the mind is out there and the body is out there, and you are not the mind, you are not the body. As long as you know you are not the mind and the body, both of them can go on to their heart's content, and you know that they cannot touch you.

Comments:

What do you long for? Are you longing for a new car, financial security, the perfect relationship, or simply to get out of your pain? Take an inventory of your desires and you will see what is your highest priority. If there are external desires, allow yourself to honor and fulfill them and/or just let them go. If you deny what you truly desire, it has you. It is a stuckness in your consciousness that you will keep coming back to, yet, if you acknowledge it, you have the ability to either bring it into your consciousness or let it go. Either way you are taking charge of your growth and your life.

As you start to see progress on the path, know that freedom is not for you, it is from you. The "you" that I am referring to here is the apparently limited you. Not the true limitless you that you have always been. If you get attached to or take ego credit for any of your growth you will find that it can become a sticking point. Allow the free you—the impersonal power that knows the way to be your guide—to have the credit, not you. The less you take personal credit, the more you are credited. Plus, anything that you think that you have accomplished on the path is only in the past, and if you try and return to the past you are missing the only place that true growth can take place, which is here and now.

Suggestions for the week:

Make a list of your desires and be as ruthlessly honest as you can. Go through each item on the list and ask yourself, "Can I allow myself to turn this desire into a desire for freedom?" If you can do that, allow the switch to occur naturally inside you and notice the freedom you will naturally feel from just making this inner change.

Another question you can use to help you let go of the desire is: "Would I rather have (the desire) or would I rather be free?" If you cannot change the desire or let it go, then set it up as a goal and allow yourself to accomplish it as best you can.

A third way of letting go of desire is to allow yourself to let go of wanting to change what is and allow yourself to accept it as it is as best you can. You can even ask yourself the question: "Can I let go of wanting to change this and allow it to be as it is?" The more you accept things as they are, the more you will discover the freedom that is always here and always available to you just waiting for you to acknowledge it.

You may resonate with all three ways of letting go of desire or you may only resonate with one or two. Allow yourself to experiment with all three and then concentrate on the one that you most resonate with for the week.

Even when you do achieve any desire, notice whether the happiness is permanent or fleeting. How long are you truly happy with your new toy? This will also help you to start converting all your desires into the desire for freedom, your true source of lasting, unshakable happiness.

You can also make a list of your "spiritual" accomplishments and experiences and allow yourself to let them go as best you can. The more you can let go of your past experiences and accomplishments the more you are opening yourself to having the whole pie of absolute freedom for now and all time.

The following polarities will help support you in this week' work.

• I want the world–I am the world.

- I want freedom–I am freedom.
- I accomplished this–It is not I but the Father who worketh through me.
- I accomplished this–God is the only accomplisher.
- Things need to change–All is perfect as it is.

The next seven pages of this book are designed to help you further your own exploration. You can view them as your diary of progress during the week that you are working with this session. Use the space allowed on each page to write down your gains and realizations as they happen, as well as for notes on working with the various exercises.

Day One

Day Two

Day Three

Day Four

Day Five

Day Six

Day Seven

"Some of us are seeking Happiness where it is and as a result are becoming happier. And others are seeking it blindly in the world where it is not and are becoming more frustrated."

Lester Levenson

Session 4

Happiness

I'll start with that which we're all interested in, all right? The word that I like best for our subject is happiness. When we analyze that which everyone is seeking or looking for, it is happiness, right? And when you find God, your Self, that turns out to be the ultimate happiness.

When we seek and find the full truth, the absolute truth, that again turns out to be the ultimate happiness. We're all seeking the greatest good for ourselves. The ultimate good turns out to be the ultimate happiness. Every being is seeking freedom, and complete freedom or liberation is nothing but the ultimate happiness. So, in the end, the words God, good, truth, liberation, freedom and Self turn out to be the ultimate happiness. And everyone is seeking these: good, happiness, liberation, truth, God, Self. There isn't anyone who's not seeking It. The only difference between us and others is that we're consciously seeking It in the direction where It is. The others are seeking It blindly through seeking happiness in the world and never really getting the full happiness that they're striving for. We go after it directly. We seek for it where it is. We seek it within.

Everyone wants a continuous, constant, eternal happiness with no sorrow whatsoever, and no one is ever satisfied until he or she finds that. Everyone is seeking what we're all seeking. The major difference is that they are seeking It in the world and are frustrated, while we are seeking It within and are successfully becoming happier. When we go within, we discover that all happiness is there. The only place where we can feel happiness is right within ourselves. That is exactly where it is. Every time we attribute this happiness to something external–to a person or a thing external–we get more pain with it than we do pleasure.

Anyone disagree with that? If you have experienced enough, if you've lived long enough, and if you've examined it, you've discovered this. The happiness that we're seeking and thinking is out there external to us isn't there. The "happiness with no sorrow" can only be found by going within. Point number one.

Now, point number two is that this great happiness that we're seeking is nothing but our very own Self, our very own Beingness. Our most basic, inherent nature is this thing that we are seeking, and it is ours, here and now. We are that happiness that we are seeking, looking for it externally and not finding it there. Looking within, we discover it to be our very own Self unencumbered with our self-imposed limitations. There is not one of us who is not in direct touch with, in possession of, an infinite Beingness that's all perfect, all present, all joyous and eternal. There is not one of us who is not in direct contact with That right now! But due to wrong learning, by assuming, over the ages, concepts of limitation and by looking outwardly, we have beclouded the view. We have covered over this infinite Being that we are with concepts of, "I am this physical body," or, "I am this mind," or, "With this physical body and mind, I have heaps and heaps of problems and troubles."

So, in order to discover this truth, this unlimited Being that we are, we must quiet the mind and finally let go of the mind. And only in this way may we achieve it. The mind is nothing but the sum total of all thoughts. All thoughts are concepts of limitation. If anyone of us could stop thinking right now and remain that way, he would be an unlimited Being from this moment on. It really is that simple, though not necessarily an easy accomplishment. The job is first to undo negative thinking in order to get positive enough so that we may go in the right direction, then to drop all thinking–drop all negative and all positive thinking. When that happens, we discover that we are in the realm of knowingness, of omniscience. We have no need to think, since everything is known, and we are all joyous and totally free. Knowing everything, there's nothing to think about!

Thinking is just relating things to other things, connecting things together. Knowing everything, we know the unity, the oneness, and there's no necessity for relating things by thought. Thereby we are free, free of all concepts of separation and limitation. This leaves us free to use a mind should we want to communicate with the apparency of the world. The process of going within is a process of looking within and discovering what the mind is, of discovering that the mind is nothing but thoughts, and the thoughts are nothing but numerous concepts of limitation. We quiet the mind by letting go of these thoughts until the mind gets quiet enough so that we see the infinite Being that we are. This takes away the mist–the clouds covering this infinite Being–and leaves us totally free.

When we first see this infinite Being that we are, the job isn't finished yet; we still have the remaining habits of thought to do away with. Then, when there's no more remaining thought, subconscious and conscious (and the subconscious thoughts are the difficult ones to let go of), when there are no more thoughts, that's the end of the road of playing limited. Then we are totally free–forever! Actually, we have no choice. We are infinite Beings. If there is a choice, it can only be to choose to be limited! We have chosen to be limited to such a degree that now we are blindly behaving as though we are extremely limited Beings. Consequently, all the apparent troubles, troubles that are only an apparency, because they are assumed as real through our mind. Everything we see in the world, we see only in our mind. There's nothing but our consciousness; nothing can be seen except through our consciousness.

Whatever we see is in our consciousness is in our mind. When one begins to realize this, then one works to change one's consciousness, and, by so doing, one changes his environment. Changing one's environment is a step on the way. In doing so you have the proof; do you understand what I'm saying? Nothing should ever be accepted on hearsay.

Never believe anything you hear. If you accept what I say to you just by listening to it, it's only hearsay. You must prove everything for yourself. When you do, it's your knowledge, and it's useable. To progress in the direction of wisdom and happiness, it's absolutely necessary that everyone prove it out for himself.

As it's said above, truth can never be found in the world. The world as we see it now is multiple, dual. When we go just behind the world, we discover the absolute truth: that there's a singular Oneness throughout the world and universe, and it turns out to be our very own Self, our very own Beingness, which some call God. The world is, but not as people see it. The world is truly only our very own Self. The "I" that we use when we say, "I am," is the exact same "I," falsely appearing separate and divided. When we see the truth, we see that you are me, that there is only one Beingness, there is only one consciousness and that we are the sum total of all the Beingness or consciousness that formerly appeared separate.

So, again, to find truth or happiness, you have to go within. You have to see the Oneness, you have to see the universe as it really is, as nothing but your consciousness, which is nothing but your Self. Now, this is difficult to describe; it's something that must be experienced. Only when someone experiences it does one know. It cannot be picked up from listening to anyone. Books and teachers can only point the direction; we must take it. That's one of the nice things about the path. There's nothing to be believed–everything must be experienced and proved by each one to his own satisfaction before it's accepted.

To sum it up, I can take two quotes from the Bible: "I am that I am" and "Be still and know that I am God." In other words, "Thou art that which thou art seeking." Quiet the mind until you see it. Okay? Now we may go into questions.

Q: I come upon a difference: these people, all of us in this room, each of us has a form, and I see it.

Lester: You're seeing wrongly. You're seeing in error. When you look at me, you should see the truth, you should see your Self. Strive until that day in which you will see this truth.

Q: After one has a certain amount of inner experience and begins to believe, there still comes an important decision as to what to do with yourself as you find yourself at that point. And then you have to decide what to do with the rest of your life.

Lester: Yes. You must decide whether to pursue your welfare by seeking it in the world or by seeking it within you.

Q: You've had a certain amount of experience, but you will always be called back to a certain contact with the outer world unless–

Lester: Unless you make the outer world you. However, be not attached to the world and it cannot disturb you. Then you may carry on with equanimity.

Q: In order to make the outer world me, I would think I have to self-purify myself.

Lester: Yes. Practicing serving the world will purify you.

Q: I would have to almost go out and sacrifice what remains of myself in some kind of service.

Lester: The only thing you will ever sacrifice in this direction is your misery. Rendering service would give only happiness, to the degree your heart is in it. The more you willingly serve the world, the more you discover that you are related to everything and everyone. There is no isolation. It is serving and becoming the All that should be our direction. You don't cut out and let others be separate from you. You become them through the practice of serving them.

Q: The only reason I would make an effort in this direction is so I could better help other people.

Lester: Good, but you can't help other people any more than you can help yourself. So, the best way to help others is to help yourself. It's automatically so that you'll help others to the degree that you'll help yourself. Do both.

Q: So help yourself by helping others? Isn't it a two-way action?

Lester: Yes. However, it's the motive that counts. If I'm helping you with selfish motives, it doesn't help you or me. If I help only to help you, I grow. But there are many people in the world who help for their own ego-glorification, and it doesn't help them any; nor does it help you, because they then help you ego-wise, i.e., they help validate your ego.

Q: That's a very subtle thing, a very difficult thing to get rid of, that ego.

Lester: Right. When there's no more ego, the only thing left is the infinite Being that you are. Ego is the sense of separation from the All. I am an individual, Lester, and I am separate from the All, and all you people are other than I. That is the sense of ego, separateness. The moment I'm not the All, I lack something, and then I try to get it back. I think I need the missing parts of the All, and I start trying to get them. Thus, I assume I don't have the All, I am limited, and this starts a downward spiral, and we continue until we get where we are.

However, we're all on the way up now. And the big problem is to get rid of our ego, the sense that I am an individual separate from everything. We can do this by looking at our motivations. When our motivation is selfish, we change it, make it altruistic. When we act for others rather than for ourselves, in this way we grow.

Q: Is growth a constant becoming aware?

Lester: Yes. You must first want to. When you want to, then you do become aware of your thinking. Then you become aware of your non-thinking, which shows up as periods of peace and well-being.

Q: Like trying to find out, for instance, why one feels things, or why one is sick, like these past two years of illness for me. It's tremendous, Lester. Even this morning when I was talking to my sister on the telephone, after speaking to her, I kept thinking, "Why? Why? Why?" and I tried to be still–as still as I could possibly be. All of a sudden, a realization of the why I had been so negative came to me with such tremendous clarity. And I thought of you so intensely and I thought, "Well, this is what Lester possibly means." It's finding out the why, and when one sees it, one immediately turns it into something positive, and one is released.

Lester: Right, very good. Keep that up until there is no more.

Q: That's what you always meant about making the subconscious thought conscious and then letting go of it.

Lester: Yes. Pulling the subconscious thought up into consciousness, and, when it's there, you'll see it and naturally let go of it because of its negativity. But as long as it remains unconscious, you don't see it and can't do anything about it, can you?

Q: No. And tremendous things come up when one begins. Wow! Alligators! It's not easy.

Lester: Ego-wise, you don't like what comes up, and you tend to fight it.

Q: Many times I go along on an even keel, and then something comes up in personal relationships or from other directions; all of a sudden you feel a severe pain, and then you realize that any time you feel pain, you're showing your own limitation, and you step back, look at it and release yourself from the whole situation.

Lester: Yes, every situation can be used for growth by observing what's going on, the way you do. DO THIS ALL THE TIME, until there is no more needed to be let go of, until there is no more ego.

Q: Creative work, for instance, has the ego involved in that, too. It's very subtle. And the more one sees spiritually, the more one is able to paint a picture, or make music or whatever one does. This is a point that has always bothered me, the ego-involvement in this. It has worried me. How can one channel it, commercialize it, sell something?

Lester: The answer is simple: Commercialize it, but be not attached to this creativeness.

Q: Difficult. It's the ego saying, "I am the creator."

Lester: It doesn't matter what you do, be not attached to it. Let go of the sense of, "I am the creator." Let the creativeness flow through you.

Q: I would think that in almost any creative act, there has to be a spiritual part, the stem of it is basically some pure motivation, but it's almost always mixed with ego.

Lester: Let me clear up one thing: everything you do is creative. It's impossible to do anything that's not creative. That's because the mind is only creative; but when we create things we don't like, we call it non-creative and destructive. When we create things we like, we call that creative and constructive. But the mind only creates. Everyone is a creator. What we hold in mind, we create.

Q: So all this ego of ours is our own creation?

Lester: Right. It's better to create constructive things like beauty, health and affluence as they do not demand as much attention from us as a sick body or a sick pocketbook. Consequently, we have more time and ease to look in the direction of truth and to discover our Self.

Q: Sometimes I think that one thinks too much of the ego and then the ego grows, and you want to fight it more and you give it more importance.

Lester: Yes. But it's too well-grown right now, far more than you can see, in the unconscious part of your mind. Mind is nothing but the sum total collection of all thoughts. The unconscious part of the mind is holding all the thoughts that we are not looking at this moment. But those hundreds of thousands of thoughts are there, and they're active. Unconsciously, you're operating that body; you're operating every cell. You're working a chemical plant, a cir- culatory, a cooling and a heating system—all these thoughts are active and are actively operating your body.

Also, there are thousands of thoughts of wanting things and not wanting things, likes and dislikes. But even if they're unconscious, they're active; whether we look at them or not, they are still active, and they are sustained and motivated by our ego. This is the diffi- cult part for us, to make these ego-motivated thoughts conscious so that we may let go of them. However, someday we reach a place where we will not be that ego-mind. When we see that, "I am not that mind, I am not that body, I am not that ego," then we'll really see. And when we really see we are not that, it's possible to drop that ego-mind-body, once and for all.

Q: Because one has re-become what one is?

Lester: Not re-become, one has re-remembered, re-discovered, re-recognized what he always was.

Q: So the ego thing falls off like a crust.

Lester: Right, gone forever. Now that's what we do eventually. At first, we work at dropping the ego until we get enough attention free so that we can seek who and what we are. Then, when we see who and what we are, we say, "This is ridiculous," and we don't identify with the ego-mind-body anymore. Then we watch the body go through life like we now watch every other body. You watch it, and you know that the body is not you. You're really above that body; you're not limited or bound by it. You know you are eternal, whole, perfect and free, and you let the body go its way, like a puppet.

Q: And then you use the body for whatever you like if you want to, or, if not, the show just goes on.

Lester: Yes. You let the show go on. It's a show that you wrote called "Bodies Playing Limited." However, you are free to choose to use the body to communicate with others, to help them grow.

Q: Isn't everything we see, a piece of wood, a potato chip, part of that eternal truth?

Lester: Yes, but you have to see it as nothing but you, then you see the truth of it. The world doesn't disappear, our perception of it changes—completely. Instead of the world being other than us, it becomes us, or we become it. When you see the world as you, it will look entirely different from what it looked like when it appeared separate. You will love and identify with it and everyone in it. When you fully love someone, you identify with and you become one with that one. When you become the universe, you love the universe, or, if you fully love the universe, you become the universe. Love is absolutely necessary. When we love totally, we totally identify with the grand and glorious infinite Being that we are!

Comments:

What if we already are what we are seeking—the ultimate happiness—and even an apparently external object like a new car is not separate from us? Everything is already always being satisfied from within because we are the totality. There is no thing and no one that is separate from or outside of who we are. As you live with this idea and make this understanding your own, your life will change forever.

Suggestions for the week:

Allow yourself to explore the oneness that is already evident all around you. You can do this in any of the following ways.

Look for what is the same. The mind is expert at creating differences and at creating the apparent separation, but if you look you will be able to find that which is the same in everything you experience. Start with the obvious similarities like, "I am a human. He or she is a human," and then allow yourself to be taken deeper to the deepest underlying unity.

Practice seeing you—Beingness—everywhere you look. Start by seeing other people as you—Beingness. Then other things as you—Beingness—and finally it will lead you to seeing every atom as you. Also make sure to focus on that which surrounds and interpenetrates all that appears. It is often easier to see this underlying unity when you focus on the emptiness or the vastness that allows all the apparent diversity to be.

You can also use the following polarities to aid you in your self-discovery:

- I am the creator–God is the only creator.
- Happiness can be achieved–Happiness is already my basic nature.
- I am the body and the mind–I am more than just a body and a mind.
- I am different from you–I am the same as you.
- There is a me and a you–There is no me and you. There is only one.

The next seven pages of this book are designed to help you further your exploration. You can view them as your diary of progress during the week that you are working with this session. Use the space allowed on each page to write down your gains and realizations as they happen, as well as for notes on working with the various exercises.

Day One

Day Two

Day Three

Day Four

Day Five

Day Six

Day Seven

"The original state for all Beings is Love.

Our troubles are due only to our covering

over this natural state."

Lester Levenson

Session 5

Love

This session is composed of aphorisms compiled from various talks by Lester. Allow yourself to ponder them one at a time. Give yourself enough time to gain the maximum benefit that each has to offer before moving on to the next.

- Human love is that which most people think love is. Real, divine love, however, is a constant, persistent acceptance of all beings in the universe—fully, wholly, totally—as the other beings are, and loving them because they are the way they are.

- Divine love is wanting and allowing the other one to be the way the other one wants to be. Divine love is seeing and accepting everyone equally, and I think that this is the test of how divine our love is. Is it the same for every person we meet? Is our love for those who are opposing us as strong as for those who are supporting us?

- Real, divine love is unconditional and is for everyone alike. The greatest example of it is Christ with His teachings of turn the other cheek, love your enemy and so forth. If we as a nation were to practice this, we could make every enemy of ours completely impotent, just by loving them. They would be powerless to do any harm to us. However, we would have to do it as a nation, at least the majority of the people would have to love their enemy.

- Real love itself is something we can't turn on and off. Either we have it or we don't have it, and with it, it's impossible to love one person and hate another. To the degree that we hate anyone, to that degree we do not love the others. Our love is no greater than our hatred is for any one person.

- What most people call love is simply a need. If we say that I love this person but not the other, we feel that we need this person, and therefore we'll be nice to this person so that we can get what we want. But that's not real love.

- Human love is selfish, divine love is completely selfless. It is the selfless love that gives unlimited joy beyond our greatest imagination. Try it and discover this for yourself.

- The real love is the love we feel for others. It is determined by how much we give ourselves to others.

- Full love is identifying with every other being.

- When we identify with everyone, we treat everyone as we would treat ourselves.

- Love is the balm, the salve, that soothes and heals everything and all.

- When you love, you lift others to love.

- The most you can give is your love. It is greater than giving materially.

- When you understand people, you see that they are doing right in their own eyes. When you understand, you allow, you accept. If you understand, you love.

- When we love, not only are we happy, but our whole life is in harmony.

- Happiness is equal to one's capacity to love.

- If we love completely, we are perfectly happy.

- There is always either love or the lack of it.

- When one is not loving, one is doing the opposite.

- The highest love is when you become the other one. Identity is love in its highest form.

- If you love your enemy, you have no more enemies!

- The powerful effect of love is self-obvious. Just try it!

- If you will look at it from your very own center, the words love, acceptance, identification, understanding, communication, truth, God and Self are all the same.

- The original state of man was all love. His troubles are due only to his covering over of his natural state of love.

- Love and discover that selflessness turns out to be the greatest good for yourself.

- Love is effortless, whereas hate requires much effort.

- Apply love and every problem resolves.

- Human love is needing the other one. Divine love is giving to the other one.

- Love equals happiness. When we are not happy, we are not loving.

- The concept of possessiveness is just the opposite of the meaning of love. Love frees, possessiveness enslaves.

- Love is a feeling of oneness with, of identity with, the other one. When there's a full love, you feel yourself as the other person; then, treating the other person is just like treating your very own Self. You delight in the other's joy.

- Love is a tremendous power. One discovers that the power behind love, without question, is far more powerful than the hydrogen bomb.

- One individual with nothing but love can stand up against the entire world, because this love is so powerful. This love is nothing but the Self. This love is God.

- Love will not only give all the power in the universe, it will give all the joy and all the knowledge, too.

- The best way to increase our capacity to love is through understanding ourselves.

- I think everyone knows the wonderful experience of loving one person, so you can imagine what it's like when you love three billion people. It would be three billion times more enjoyable.

- Love is a constant attitude that evolves in us when we develop it. We should try practicing the love first on our family. Grant everyone in the family their own Beingness, then apply it to friends, then strangers, then to everyone.

- The more we practice love, the more we love; the more we love, the more we can practice love. Love begets love.

- The more we develop love, the more we come in touch with the harmony of the universe; the more delightful our life becomes, the more beautiful, the more everything it becomes. It starts a cycle going in which you spin upwards.

- The only method of receiving love is to give love, because what we give out must come back.

- The easiest thing to do in the universe is to love everyone. That is, once we learn what love is, it's the easiest thing to do. It takes tremendous effort not to love everyone, and you see the effort being expended in everyday life. But when we love, we're at one with all. We're at peace and everything falls into line perfectly.

- In the higher spiritual love, there's no self-deprivation. We don't have to hurt ourselves when we love everyone, and we don't.

- With love, there's a feeling of mutuality. That which is mutual is correct. If you love, you hold to that law.

- Love is smothered by wrong attitudes. Love is our basic nature and a natural thing, that's why it's so easy. The opposite takes effort. We move away from our natural self, cover it, smother it with concepts of the opposite of love and then, because we're not loving, unloving comes back at us.

- We feel the greatest when we love.

- The real love wins the universe—not just one person, but everyone in the universe.

- Behind the concepts of non-love, there is always the infinite love that we are. You can't increase it. All you can do is peel away the concepts of non-love and hatred so that this tremendous loving Being that we are is not hidden anymore.

- Love is an absolutely necessary ingredient on the path. If we ever expect to get full realization, we must increase our love until it is complete.

- When you really love, you can never feel parting. There is no distance, because they're right in your heart.

- Only through growth do we really understand what love is. When you really love, you understand the other one fully.

- Love is an attitude that is constant. Love doesn't vary. Love cannot be chopped up.

- All love, including human love, has its source in divine love.

- Every human being is basically an extremely loving individual.

- When you love, you think only the best for those you love.

- The more you love, the more you understand.

- There's one word that will distinguish the right love from the wrong love, and that is giving.

- You could hug a tree the same way as a person when you are very high. Your love permeates everything.

- Total self-abnegation is the most selfish thing we can do. When self-abnegation is total, we think only of others and are automatically in the Self.

- Love is the state of the Self. It is something you are.

- Consideration is a necessary part of love.

- Anything but full love is, to a degree, hate.

- Can you see why you can't be against anything? The ant is God, the enemy is God. If you're limiting any part, you're holding God away. Love cannot be parceled. Love has to be for all.

- The greatest of all progress is love.

- Your capacity to love is determined by your understanding.

- If you don't trust someone, you don't love him fully.

- If we love this world, we accept the world the way it is. We don't try to change it, we let it be. We grant the world its beingness. Trying to change others is injecting our own ego.

- The more we love, the less we have to think.

- Being love is higher than loving. The real devotee of God has no choice to love–he is love.

- Love is your Self, that is the highest love.

- Love is an attitude that is constant. Love doesn't vary. We love our family as much as we love strangers. To the degree we're capable of loving strangers, to that same degree we're capable of loving our family.

- Love is togetherness.

- Love is the Self. The Self doesn't love, the Self is love. (Only in duality can you love.)

- It's not loving, it's being love that will get you to God.

- Each one glorifies himself by service rendered to others and must, therefore, necessarily receive from others. Thus, God flows back and forth, and we delight in His exoticism. There is nothing so delectable as the spirit of givingness. It is intoxicating beyond any other experience capable to man. Discover this.

  Service is the secret to bathing in the ever-new joy of God. Service opens the doors to the greatest fields of beauty and charm wherein is enjoyed the nectars of the infinite variety of tastes all blended into one drink–that of superlative love.

Come into the garden of the most delicious and everlasting joy by an everlasting desire to love and serve. Let go of the emptiness of selfishness. Fill yourself to the fullest with selfless love.

Comments:

Lester used to say, "Every feeling except love is a non-love feeling and is therefore varying degrees of hatefulness." How loving are you? Do you have other feelings besides love? If you do, do not despair. Love is your basic nature even when you are lost in the strongest feeling or most limiting story to the opposite. All you need to do to uncover this truth within yourself is to release or let go of your non-love feelings, and what is left over is the real you, which is only love.

Suggestions for the week:

Lester used to suggest a technique that he called "Square All with Love." To experience this technique in your life, do the following: Allow yourself to begin the process of changing all your non-love feelings to love. Remember these feelings only appear to cover over your true loving nature, and as you release, the natural love that you are will come shining through more and more. Simply ask yourself, whenever you have a non-love feeling that you want to release: "Could I change this feeling to love?"

Letting go is always merely a choice, and if you allow yourself to make this choice, the non-love feeling that is appearing on the surface will dissolve, revealing the love that is always right in the background waiting to be uncovered. It is an invitation for love to dissolve whatever other feeling is on the surface.

Since love has infinite power there is no feeling that love cannot dissolve. Keep working with the same feeling until you feel only love in that situation, not the feeling with which you started out. This may seem like it will take awhile to accomplish, and sometimes it will take a few releases before it is all gone, but if you are persistent in practicing this technique you will find it goes much faster and gets much easier to do.

Start by experimenting in this exercise with feelings that are less intense and ingrained. As you practice this on the easier feelings, you will find that even your deepest hurts and disappointments can be easily released in this way.

You may also want to work with these polarities:

- I want to be loved–I allow myself to love.
- I need love–I am love.
- Could I allow myself to hate (any person, place, or thing) as much as I do?–Could I allow myself to love (any person, place, or thing) as much as I do?
- I am loving–I am love.

The next seven pages of this book are designed to help you further your own exploration. You can view them as your diary of progress during the week that you are working with this session. Use the space allowed on each page to write down your gains and realizations as they happen, as well as for notes on working with the various exercises.

Day One

Day Two

Day Three

Day Four

Day Five

Day Six

Day Seven

"Our real nature, the infinite real self that we
are, is simply us minus the mind."

Lester Levenson

Session 6

Realization

We try not to be intellectual. That knowledge may be gotten from reading books. Most of us already have the intellectual knowledge and yet are not realized. What we want is knowledge through experiencing it, through feeling it, through realizing and integrating it into our very Being.

The only knowledge that is useful for growth is the knowledge that we realize with our inner sight and feeling. As we contemplate, knowledge should fit in with our feelings, i.e., feel right and should integrate with our whole Beingness. Then, it is a realization, a revelation; then we know, and we know that we know. A realization is seeing something really for the first time, although you've heard it again and again. When it's realized, it's as though you've heard it for the first time. It's like an electric light bulb turning on in the mind, and you say, "Oh, now I see." It is something that you might have heard a hundred times before, but this time, on seeing and experiencing it, it's a realization. It has become real to you.

This perceived and experienced knowledge is the only

knowledge that does us any good. We can read everything on the subject, but it doesn't help. Our life doesn't change much, and it doesn't because we don't integrate the knowledge into our being-ness through realization. Realized knowledge is nonintellectual, although the means we use are intellectual. We use our mind, we direct our mind toward the answer, but you will discover that the answer does not come from the mind. It comes from a place just behind the mind. It comes from the realm of knowingness, the realm of omniscience. By quieting the mind through stilling our thoughts, each and every one of us has access to this realm of knowingness. Then and there you realize, you make real. You know and you know that you know. Is there any question about what I've just said?

Q: Are knowingness and feelingness the same thing?

Lester: No. The feeling comes just before the knowing.

Q: Is knowingness beyond feeling? Is knowledge that which feels true?

Lester: The answer to both your questions is "Yes." It's something you'll have to experience. There's a feel to things, and also there are times when you just know and you know you know, and there's no feeling to it. Knowing is really a higher level. We start with reason-ing, thinking, in the realm of thinkingness. Then we move into the realm of feelingness. The top realm is the realm of knowingness.

Q: Is ego implied in feeling?

Lester: Yes. The ego does the feeling. It is a higher ego state. Therefore, there's duality: "I" feel "emotion." Knowingness is awareness. When I said, "You know and you know that you know," you're aware, and you're aware of the fact that you are aware. There's nothing conditioning it. The very top state is the state of all awareness, of all Beingness. Beingness and awareness turn out to be the same thing when we get there. Before, it seemed as though they were two different things. But when we move to the top, Beingness, awareness and consciousness are all the same thing, because the awareness you are aware of is of Beingness being all Beingness. We see that we are not only this body, but that we are every other body, every other thing, every atom in this universe. So, if we are every being and atom, we are all Beingness.

Q: You mean I am That?

Lester: Yes, definitely! It's "I!" The top state is "I." That's all, not even "am." Just below the top, it's "I am." A step below that is "I am that I am." A step below that is "I am unlimited." A step below that is "I am great."

Q: Or one with God?

Lester: Well, where is "One with God?" One with God is not a top state because it's in duality. If I am one with God, there is "I" and "God." In the ultimate, we discover that "I" is God, there's only a singular Oneness in the universe, and we are, we must necessarily be, that Oneness. That's what we discover at the end of the line, or the beginning of the line, whichever way you look at it.

We are unlimited Beings covering over this limitlessness with concepts of limitation, the first of which is "I am an individual separate from the All." That's the very first and a very big error that we make. "I am separate, I am a personality, my name is Lester, I have a body," and I spiral right down. After we assume a mind and a body, then we assume all these troubles and all these problems, and they're nothing but assumptions. They are only a fiction that we see after we go within, quiet the mind and discover all this truth right there.

This whole world, as now seen, is nothing but a dream illusion that never was. The truth is just behind the outward world. So why make trouble? The growth is simply the elimination of all the concepts of limitation. That infinite, perfect Being that we are must always be infinite and perfect and therefore is perfect right now. That's one thing we can never change—our unlimited Self. That is all the time. But I, the unlimited Self, can assume that I am limited and that I have a mind, I have a body, I have problems. However, it is only an assumption.

Q: What's the technique for cutting through all that, for getting right to that state where you have that total awareness?

Lester: Pose the question, "Who and what am I?" and await the answer to present itself. The thinking mind can never give the answer, because all thought is of limitation. So, in quietness and meditation, pose the questions, "Who am I?" and "What am I?" When other thoughts come up, strike them down. If you can't, ask, "To whom are these thoughts? Well, these thoughts are to me. Well, then, who am I?" and you're right back on the track of "Who am I?"

Continue this until you get the answer to the question "Who and what am I?" regardless of how long it takes.

The answer is the unlimited Self. The only way It becomes obvious is when the mind stills almost completely. The only obstacles to immediate full realization here and now are the thoughts, every one of which is limited. Eliminate those thoughts and you'll see this infinite Being that you always were and are and always will be.

The difficulty is the past habit patterns of thought, the uncon-scious constant turning and churning of thought in a mechanism we have set up that we call the unconscious mind. The unconscious thoughts are simply our thoughts now that we do not look at, so we call them unconscious. This is the enemy we set up. To lessen these unconscious thoughts, we first make them conscious. When we make them conscious, then we may let go of them, and they are done forever. This quiets the unconscious mind. Now, the more we eliminate the thoughts, the more obvious our real Self becomes. The more obvious our real Self becomes, the more we are able to scorch the remaining thoughts until the mind is totally quieted.

Q: You have to still the conscious thoughts before you can get to the unconscious thoughts?

Lester: The conscious thought is only the unconscious thought made conscious.

Q: They come through dreams, too, at that state don't they, the unconscious thoughts?

Lester: Yes, but it's only in the waking state that we can eliminate them and thereby grow.

Q: You still your conscious thoughts through meditation, other techniques, etc. Now the "Who am I?" will go right through both, is that correct?

Lester: Yes. Also, you can use "Who am I?" to still or eliminate thoughts. Pose the question, "Who am I?" and when a thought comes up you say, "To whom is this thought?" The answer is, "To me." Ask, "Well, who am I?" and you're back on the track. Thus, you eliminate the thoughts as they come up.

Q: But what keeps the unconscious thoughts from popping up at that time?

Lester: They will and should pop up. If they pop up, they're conscious. Then you can drop them. Eventually you eliminate all of them.

Q: How many minds do we have?

Lester: There's only one mind. What we are looking at this moment is what the world calls the conscious mind. The part of the mind we're not looking at this moment the world calls the unconscious mind. It's the mode of mind that we give a different name to. That which we are talking about now, that which we are aware of now, is what we call the conscious mind, the conscious thought.

The unconscious mind is all the thoughts we are not interested in at this moment. What some call superconscious thought, there's really no such thing as superconscious thought. The superconscious, that which is above consciousness, is already out of the thinking realm–that's the omniscience, that's the realm of knowingness. The superconscious realm is all awareness, all knowingness. There is no thinking when you know.

Q: Is unconscious different from subconscious?

Lester: Subconscious and unconscious are the same.

Q: Do you agree with Jung's collective unconscious theory?

Lester: I only agree with truth. And this is one thing I emphasize: TRUTH IS THE ONLY AUTHORITY FOR TRUTH. Accept nothing until you can prove it out. Don't even accept what I say, no matter how much I speak as though I know. If it doesn't fit into your knowingness at present, you can accept it for checking. But only that which you can prove out for yourself, only that should you accept.

This is basically important. IT IS ABSOLUTELY NECESSARY TO PROVE ALL THIS KNOWLEDGE FOR YOURSELF. Otherwise, it's hearsay to you. You must make this knowledge your knowledge. Now, there's only one truth, one absolute truth. So putting names to it doesn't mean anything. Whether so-and-so said it, or I said it doesn't mean anything. Is it true? Does it integrate into your understanding? That's the only thing that matters. That's the point wherein we are different. We try to make this very practical so that you can use this knowledge and move toward the total understanding as quickly as possible.

Q: Is it necessary to go through stages?

Lester: No. How long should it take Infinite Power, Infinite Knowledge, to know that It is infinite?

Q: Wouldn't take any time.

Lester: Right. When man so wills with full intensity of will, it happens quickly. If you would want this more than anything else, you would have it in a matter of weeks or months.

Q: Is there any way of making yourself want it more and more?

Lester: Yes, make yourself want it by experiencing the wonderfulness of it, or make yourself more and more miserable. Well, there are two incentives: misery is one, but not the best. The sweetness of it, the wonderfulness of it, the glory of it should make us want it more than the misery should.

Q: The glory in what sense?

Lester: The glory of it, of knowing what you are. It's a tremendous experience, it's an ecstasy, a euphoria. There are no real words to describe it, because, well, we're in an age where these things are not experienced and therefore not understood, so how can there be words for things that are not understood? There are no words to describe these feelings, they're so beyond present understanding. So you pick the words you know best to describe it and that's it.

Paramhansa Yogananda uses the words "ever-new joy welling

up every second," and that's a practical way of describing it. At first, it's a joy that spills over every second, just keeps pouring out, pouring out–you feel as though you can't contain it. Later on, it resolves itself into a very profound peace, the most peaceful peace you could ever imagine. It's a delicious peace that is far more comfortable than ever-new joy. But please, get the ever-new joy!

Q: But don't stay there.

Lester: That's it. It's very easy to get stuck in the ever-new joy state. That's what they call the ananda sheath. It's the last veil we have to remove. It is the last wall we must break through. When you start this ever-new joy, it's so good you just want to continue it. Also, you have no feeling of need to change, everything is so wonderful. But it isn't the final state. The final state is the peace that passeth all understanding. It's a deep, deep peace. You move in the world, the body moves, but you have absolute peace all the time. Bombs could be dropping all around you, and you have that perfect peace regardless of what's going on.

Q: How do you maintain that state?

Lester: If you get it, you don't have to maintain it, because you have it–you are it.

Q: Well, in that particular state, then, you are really omniscient and all the other things, and there's no necessity for thinking.

Lester: Right. That's the top state. Now, it is possible to dip into this state to a certain depth that's very deep and not maintain it because of the habits from the past. The habits of thoughts that have not been eliminated re-emerge and take over. We can feel this infinite Being that we are, and it's a wonderful experience, then, the next minute, "Oh, so-and-so wants me to do this, and I don't want to do it." A thought comes in, and there you are, identifying with unhappy limitedness. You, the Self, are trying to be this unlimited Being through a very narrow ego, a very limited ego, and it hurts. That's all it is.

Q: How do you bombard that ego and get rid of it?

Lester: First and foremost, with an intense desire to let go of the ego. Second, listening to someone who knows the way and following through on the direction, especially if that one is a fully realized Being.

Q: That's hard to find.

Lester: No, they are available right where you are. Wherever you are, they're right there. I can name some of them: Jesus, Buddha, Yogananda. I don't know of any in the United States in physical body. India has, I believe, several. But there is no need for a physical body when you can get the others wherever you are, because they're omnipresent. All you need to do is open your mind's eye and see them. They're omnipresent, so they must be right where you are.

Also, they, wanting to help you, must necessarily come to you if you open yourself to them. They have no choice. They have made a commitment. So all you need to do is to ask for their help and guidance and open yourself to it, and it is there. However, since we think we're physical bodies, sometimes we more readily accept a fully realized Being when He is in a physical body. Therefore, we will take more help because, in our physical sensing He seems to be more real. Because of that, it's good to have a fully realized Being in the flesh. However, if we don't have one, it doesn't mean we can't take the guidance of those who are omnipresent.

Q: Some aspect of the Hindu thought says you can't do it without a live guru, but I think they've evolved beyond that now, and you're confirming it.

Lester: Yes. However, a guru is alive, whether in physical body or not.

Q: Do people need a live guru?

Lester: People need a guru, a teacher. He doesn't necessarily have to be alive in a physical body, but he has to be accepted as being alive. He doesn't have to be in a physical body. The reason why we need a guru is that we are in a very difficult age. It's an age of materialism where everything, everyone, is shouting at us, "This is a material world. This is it!" We have been in this world again and again and again, so we really need the assistance of a fully realized Being to offset that constant weight of the world that says we are physical, limited bodies. We should want the truth more than we want air. Then we would get full realization very quickly.

Q: Did you coin that? Is that yours, an aphorism?

Lester: Nothing is mine. Anything I say will have always been said before. I might just twist the words around this way or that way in my own style, but there's nothing new. Truth always was and always will be.

There's a story in the Eastern writings of a master and his disciple. They were bathing in the Ganges, and the disciple asked, "Master, how can I know the truth?" And the teacher took him by the hair and held him under the water until he was about ready to go unconscious. Then he let him up and said, "Now, when you want truth as much as you wanted air, then you'll have it."

They have some great stories. That snake and the rope story is an excellent analogy of the physical world. I guess everyone knows that, don't they? A person walks along the road at dusk and sees a rope on the ground, mistakes it for a snake, goes into an intense fear and a complete involvement as to what to do about this awful snake. Well, the snake is only an illusion. The real thing is a rope. So he spends a lifetime of maybe sixty-five years struggling and fighting this snake-world and then takes a rest on the astral side and comes back and fights it again and again and again until he wakes up to the fact that the snake was only the rope, and it really never was. And that's exactly what happens to this physical world. It's just like that snake: it's an illusion.

The example I like best is that what goes on in this world is exactly the same as what goes on in a night dream. While we're in the night dream, it's very real—we are there, there are other characters, it's either beautiful or ugly, and, when it's a nightmare, we're being killed. It's a real struggle. All the time we're in the dream, it is real to us. But when we awaken we say, "Oh, my gosh, it was only a dream; it never really was." And that's exactly what happens when we wake up out of this waking state dream of the world.

Comments:

Would you rather believe in freedom or be the freedom that you have always believed in? Most of us substitute belief for direct experience and knowing, which could lead us to the recognition of being. I highly recommend that you shed your beliefs and not settle for anything except the real thing.

Suggestions for the week:

Self-inquiry is a great way to be the truth, and I highly recommend that you explore it this week. In coming chapters we will explore it in greater depth, but for now allow yourself to explore it in just the way Lester described in this chapter. You may also want to add another question to your repertoire. After you ask yourself, "Who or what am I?" whatever answer arises you can follow with, "If I am more than that, what am I? … And if I am even more than that what am I?" Keep going until you just rest as That.

Another great way to experience and be the truth of who you are is by shedding the beliefs about this truth that you have accumulated since you have been on the path. Most of us have heard a tremendous amount about what is true and what is not and most of us have accepted much on hearsay before we proved it out for ourselves. Anything that we accept on hearsay can act as powerful obstruction to direct experience.

This simple process will allow you experience, realize, and then be the truth, rather than just believe it. Make a list of your spiritual beliefs and then use any of the following questions to let them go.

The first question is quite direct. Simply ask yourself: "Could I let go of this belief?" and then do your best to just let it go. The more you let it go of the belief, the more you will uncover what is true.

Another question you can use is: "Would I rather believe in (the belief) or would I rather know the truth?" Or similarly: "Would I rather believe in (the belief)· or would I rather be the truth?" You can use either of these questions interchangeably and they will have the same effect of dissolving the belief and revealing the underlying truth.

You may also want to use these polarities:

- I know this–This is merely a belief.
- This is the truth–This is a belief.
- This is real–This is merely a belief.
- I know the truth–I am the truth.

The next seven pages of this book are designed to help you further your exploration. You can view them as your diary of progress during the week that you are working with this session. Use the space allowed on each page to write down your gains and realizations as they happen, as well as for notes on working with the various exercises.

Day One

Day Two

Day Three

Day Four

Day Five

Day Six

Day Seven

"'Love' and 'giving' are two words that are synonymous. It's in the spirit of givingness that the secret to joy lies."

Lester Levenson

Session 7

Love, Giving and the Christ Consciousness

It is now the Christmas season; so let us direct our attention toward Christmas. Maybe I ought to allow you to lead me into what you would like to hear about Christmas—or should I just talk? All right.

Christ-mass, the day when the masses look toward Christ, when mass is held in reverence to Jesus. When I interpret the Bible, it's the way I see it, not the way I've read it or someone else has said it's so. Christmas is related to Christ. Christ is not the man Jesus. Christ is the title of Jesus who has attained the Christ Consciousness. And I think if you separate the two, Jesus and Christ, you will far better understand the meaning of His words and the meaning of the Bible. When He says, "I am the way," He doesn't mean Jesus, He means Christ. So, first I'd better explain what I mean by Christ and Jesus.

Jesus was a man who was born on this earth approximately 2,000 years ago, who, through righteousness, or right-useness, rightly used the world to attain the Christ Consciousness. In so doing,

He showed the way to immortality that each and every one of us must take. We must die to death, i.e., eliminate from our consciousness all thoughts of death and hold in its place only eternality and immortality. In order to show us, He allowed Himself to be crucified so that He could prove immortality by resurrecting Himself. He was a way-shower and dedicated and gave His life only to show us the way.

Christ Consciousness is the consciousness that saves us from all this mess that we find ourselves in when we try to be worldly man. It is the attaining of the Christ Consciousness that saves us from all the horrors and miseries of the world. It is the Christ Consciousness that gives us liberation from all difficulty and leads us into our immortality. If we were to try to be Jesus, we would have all the trials and tribulations that He went through. However, when we become the Christ, by being Christ-like and thereby attaining the Christ Consciousness, we eliminate all and every misery and have nothing but infinite joy.

So, Christhood is a state that was attained by the man Jesus. He attained His Christhood before He was born, and He came back to show us the way by actual example. And if you will keep these two in their meaning as you read the Bible, I believe it will make much more sense. Christmas is known mostly by the spirit of givingness, of good will toward all men. Locked up in that word "givingness" is the key to all happiness. It's in the spirit of givingness that we have and experience the greatest joy. If you'll think back, you'll see that when you were giving, you were most joyous.

"Love" and "giving" are two words that are synonymous. It's in the spirit of givingness that the secret to joy lies. When we fully have that, we want to give everything that we have to everyone we meet, and we have infinite joy. It's so important. It's in the spirit of givingness, it's not in the givingness of things, unfortunately, because Christmas is a great time of gift-giving. People are giving, giving, giving. But it's not in the givingness—it's in the spirit of givingness that the joy lies. The feeling of the spirit of givingness is felt more around Christmastime by more people than any other time of the year. It's a wonderful thing. We should make every day Christmas. When we get full realization, we do just that. There isn't a moment in which we're not wanting to give everything we know to everyone.

Q: You mean giving things, or giving of yourself?

Lester: Well, first givingness. If we give with strings attached, with reservations, with recriminations, there is little joy in it. But when we give freely, we have the greatest of feelings, and it's this constant spirit of givingness that is the secret of eternal joy.

Now, the greatest thing we can give, as the Bible says, is wisdom, because when you give one wisdom, you give one the method of attaining everything, not just one single thing. So, the greatest of all givingness is giving wisdom, is giving understanding, is giving knowledge of this subject that we are interested in.

I might explain it this way. If you give a man a meal when he's hungry, he's made happy for the moment, and he's satisfied. But three hours later he needs another meal, and probably thousands of meals after that. So what is one meal that you give to him? Relatively little. However, if you give the man the understanding of how to produce a meal, he will never go hungry! You will give him the knowledge of how to always have all the food he wants. You will have given him sixty thousand meals! So, that's the greatest giving-ness, giving understanding and wisdom.

Practicing this would be an excellent method of growth, and, I think as a group you're ready for it. Give this understanding to everyone whom you meet who asks for it. It's excellent in that it takes you out of your little self onto others. It's an act of love. I'm suggesting that this givingness be taken on as almost a way of life from here on to help others to get this understanding. It will help you to rapidly attain mastership, and it will give you the greatest of all joys. It's good to give gifts. They should be given from the heart. However, I think we are all at the point where we can give much more than just things. We should try to give wisdom and under-standing. Did I answer your question?

Q: Yes.

Q: This is only if we are asked?

Lester: Yes. If we try to help people who are not asking for it, we are just expressing our own ego. "I know something you should know," see? "I" talking down to "you," trying to teach you something when you're not asking for it, is just ego-expression on my part, so it should only be given when asked for.

Q: Is there a time when you become sensitive enough so that you do say things to people that they need, even without them asking?

Lester: Yes, there is. As you let go of your ego, you automatically tune in more with others. The less your ego, the more you are attuned to others. You reach a state in which they don't even have to ask. You'll discover that some people who ask don't really want help. Likewise, some people who say, "I don't want any help" are really wanting it.

It takes a little experience to handle situations like that. But it's true that as we grow, as we let go of our ego, we become more attuned to others, and we automatically help them. And we help at all times, no matter what or where a situation is. It could be the cashier in a market or someone you meet on the street. There's always a certain givingness that should be going on all the time. And it doesn't have to be only words of wisdom, it could be a kind word, an expression of love. It wouldn't hurt to try helping others. That would be the greatest of all givingness. Any more questions?

Q: What is the second coming of the Christ?

Lester: The second coming of the Christ is not the same as the second coming of Jesus. The second coming of Jesus will be the time when He returns and walks on this earth again in a physical body. I believe it will be the body that He had the last time He walked the earth. The second coming of the Christ is when we attain the Christ Consciousness.

As a group, we are very fortunate in that we are close to Jesus. This was very evident the very first time we had a meditation when Jesus came into this room and walked around to almost every one here. It was a very definite and a very important sign that, as a group, Jesus is very interested in us, is trying to help us with all the power that He has. That power is never given unless we are receptive to it. There's no forcing it. He can only use His power when we open ourselves to Him. If and when we do, He is right there, ready and very capable. Just try Him.

We need this direct connection with a master if we want to go all the way this lifetime. As I've said, it's so difficult in these times to achieve mastership that it is necessary to have this connection with a master, so that when we are ready to leave this plane, he will assist us in getting full realization. There isn't anyone in this room who cannot make it this lifetime, if he or she will just stay faithful to the path until the end. Every one of us can make it this lifetime if we really want it.

Q: Will you define "making it"?

Lester: Christhood and full realization. "Making it" is becoming a master. What is a master? A master is one who is master over all matter in the universe and who is master over his mind. A master is one who sees his own infinity right within him. A master is one who has undone all thoughts of limitation, who has ripped off all these sheaths of limitations and is free.

Q: And this we can do in this lifetime?

Lester: Yes, definitely! You must want it more than anything else. You must want it more than you want things of the world. And if you do, when you're ready to leave this place, you'll get the assistance from the master that you look to, and he will help you over. The way he will do it is this way: If you don't make it before you die, you will make it at the time of your so-called death. When a person dies, all thoughts of this lifetime and all thoughts of prior lifetimes come up for review. The master identifies with us. He sees us as himself, and as these thoughts come up in our mind, it's like coming up in his mind, and he, identified with and as us, helps us undo them. When they are totally undone, we are totally free!

Q: This is what we are doing every day when we say, "We're not limited. I won't accept this. I'm not this limited being." Isn't this what we should be doing all day long?

Lester: Yes. We should continue it until the end of all thoughts. We should not be limited by any thing or any thought.

Q: But this is jumping so far. I'm interested in being able to walk down the street without getting mad at the fellow in front of me.

Lester: I'm trying to show you the entire way. What I'm trying to do is to give you a map that takes you all the way. I'm not saying, "Bob, be this today." But I think if you have a map that shows the entire route, you can take it all by yourself. You don't need to have people like me say this to you. Once you've got the map, all you need to do is to follow it. I'm trying to give you a complete picture, a complete understanding of what full realization is and the way to accomplish it. And it's a very difficult thing to do, because you'll never really know what it is until you attain it.

Q: And the ego is simply the feeling that I am not this.

Lester: Right. The ego is a feeling that I am a separate individual, separate from the All, and I need a body and a mind to be separate.

Q: That's limited?

Lester: Well, if I have a body, and I have a mind, I have thousands of limitations. I have to feed the body, take care of it. I have thoughts. My feelings are hurt. This goes on and on and on. Realize what you are. You'll see that you are not the body, you are not the ego. Discover what you are and be infinite.

Q: Can Jesus save us?

Lester: Jesus doesn't save, the Christ Consciousness saves. We should believe not in Jesus but believe as Jesus believed. When we make an effort to attain the Christ Consciousness, Jesus helps us to realize it. Jesus is always available to anyone who asks and is receptive to His help. You may and can contact Jesus to the degree you actually accept the fact that you can. Were you to accept that you could talk to Jesus in a physical body, then you would meet with Him in a physical body. If you can accept meeting with Him in a vision or in a dream, then you would meet with Him in that manner. If you can accept Him as a presence, then you will feel His presence and receive His support. It is all up to you.

Comments:

Do you live every day with the same feeling of givingness as you do, at times, during the Christmas season? What is standing in your way? You will discover as you allow yourself to explore givingness in your heart that your heart overflows with the love that you are. The more giving you feel, the more you will feel that you already have everything that you need or want for yourself, and the more your world will reflect that. The expression, "The giver is blessed," refers to one who gives without wanting something back in return. Just the feeling alone that comes from giving freely is exquisite, let alone whatever else comes back to you. But this can happen only if you give from your heart without wanting anything back in return.

Suggestions for the week:

Practice giving without wanting anything in return. This is something that you can do all day every day with everyone you meet. Start by giving everyone you meet your love, compassion, and understanding. This is more than enough. You can also share with them what you are learning from this course. And if you are able, also give what is needed on a physical level.

When you give, make sure that you give to those who want to receive. Refrain from forcing those who are not interested. Also allow yourself to feel that the person to whom you are giving is your equal and is already whole, complete, and perfect, as opposed to being in need. The highest gift you can give anyone is to grant him or her their Beingness–to see them as they truly are. The more you give without wanting anything back in return, the more your heart will overflow with love and your life will be filled with the abundance of the universe.

If the giving does not bring with it a feeling of joy, it is because there are strings attached to your gift. To keep yourself honest, you can make a list of what you have given that day and then check to see if you wanted anything back in return. If you were, simply ask yourself, "Could I let go of wanting anything back in return for this gift?" This will help free you of the strings that you have attached to your giving and will open up the universal flow.

You can also do this exercise on any of your past gifts that you remember.

You may also want to experiment with these polarities:

- I am the giver–God is the only giver.
- Could I allow my gifts to be as conditional as they are? – Could I allow them to be as unconditional as they are?
- I want something back in return–I have all I need and want nothing back in return.
- I own this–It is a gift from God.

The next seven pages of this book are designed to help you further your exploration. You can view them as your diary of progress during the week that you are working with this session. Use the space allowed on each page to write down your gains and realizations as they happen, as well as for notes on working with the various exercises.

Day One

Day Two

Day Three

Day Four

Day Five

Day Six

Day Seven

The Next Steps

Congratulations on completing Book 1 of *Happiness Is Free*. As you apply what you have learned to your quest for the ultimate happiness, you should find your apparent problems dropping away and your natural freedom shining forth. This will continue until you are at rest in every moment as the Beingness that you have always been and you see the exquisite perfection of All That Is.

The following suggestions are designed to help you get the maximum benefit from the material in this book on an ongoing basis:

1. Allow yourself to use the material in every part of your life. If you only thought about and explored freedom for a few minutes a day, you would gain tremendous benefits. However, if you allowed freedom to be in your mind and heart throughout the day, those results would increase exponentially. Like everything else, the more energy you put into the process, the more you get out of it.

2. Review the material often. Every time you reread and work with the ideas in this book, you will get more out of them. As you mature spiritually, you will understand and be able to apply what you learn on deeper levels. Treat each review as though it were your first time. Explore all the exercises, and allow a full week for each session.

3. Share what you have learned. Communicating these ideas and practices with your friends, relatives, and acquaintances should stretch you and deepen your own understanding. Additional benefits come from surrounding yourself with like-minded people who are also interested in deepening their freedom. However, please remember only to share this material with those who are truly interested in hearing about it. Grant those you know their Beingness–see them as already perfect–whether or not they share your interest.

4. Start or join a *Happiness Is Free* support group. An energetic lift comes "when two or more are gathered in thy name." The larger the group, the more this energetic lift is magnified. Lester used to say that the energy in groups is "squared." In other words, two people have the power of two times two, three people have the power of three times three, and so on. Another benefit of participating in a group is seeing the material from perspectives other than your own. This can deepen your understanding. (See p. 188, Guidelines for *Happiness Is Free* Support Groups.)

5. Read the other four books in this series. Together they comprise a total of thirty-five sessions. Each book, in and of itself, is a complete course on the ultimate happiness. But if you have enjoyed reading and working with this one, you would probably enjoy and benefit from the other books as well.

6. Learn the Sedona Method®. As we have already mentioned, Lester's material truly comes alive when it is combined with the Sedona Method®. Lester was so excited about this part of his teaching that he devoted the last twenty years of his life to perfecting and promoting it. There are two great ways to learn the Sedona Method®. You can explore the power of letting go through live seminars, which are offered worldwide, or in audiotape programs.

To get information on the Sedona Method® Course, you may visit the Sedona Training Associates website: **www.sedona.com**, e-mail us at **release@sedona.com**, or call us at **(928) 282-3522**. At the end of this book there is a fill-out form that you can also use to request further information.

7. Review and deepen your use of Holistic Releasing™. The Holistic Releasing™ process is an integral part of this book. If you have enjoyed working with the polarities at the end of the sessions, you would probably also enjoy our tape programs *Practical Freedom* and *Absolute Freedom* or attending a seminar on this technique. (See the contact information above.)

You are the key to your own happiness. All you need to do is use that key to unlock the secrets of freedom and happiness that are waiting to be discovered right within your own heart. Good luck and enjoy.

Guidelines for *Happiness Is Free* Support Groups

The goal of a group should be to support each participant in gaining the most they can from their use of the material. It is important that a safe space be created so that everyone feels free to participate, yet never feels pressured to do so. This is best facilitated if a different member of the group is given an opportunity to be the leader each time the group meets, if they chose to do so. It helps to prevent one person from dominating the group. It also allows participants to stretch in the direction of helping others.

If anyone brings up an emotional or physical issue that would usually be handled by a trained medical professional, they should be encouraged to seek a health professional. These support groups should never be used as a substitute for competent medical attention. They should be used as an aid to each participant's personal and spiritual growth.

It is helpful to have the support group meet once a week since each session is designed to be used for a full week. If at first that is difficult, meeting once a month would still be helpful.

If you are using private residences for your meetings, it is also helpful to rotate the location where the support group is being held so that the burden for hosting is not borne by only one person. However, if you can find a centrally located free public location we encourage you to use it on an ongoing basis.

The following instructions are for the leader of the support group.

Welcome Everyone

Start with a brief quote from Lester from the week's session. Then allow for a few minutes of silence to give everyone an opportunity to ponder the quote and to get centered and present in the room. Do your best to create the safe space for everyone attending.

Ice Breaker

Have the group share their names and a gain that they have experienced so far from *Happiness Is Free*.

Partner Work

Have each person in the group find a partner and support each other in doing an exercise from the week's session. Select an exercise that would be appropriate to do with a partner from the book. Spend approximately thirty minutes on the exercise, either having the partners switch back and forth, taking turns facilitating each other, or time it so each participant has about fifteen minutes to do their exploration with the support of their partner.

Have each partner open their copy of *Happiness Is Free* to the exercise being explored, so they can remember the verbiage and remind each other to change the wording to the third person using the pronoun "you" instead of "I."

Read the Following Statement Aloud

Be there with and for your partner as best you can. Grant them their Beingness by allowing them to have their own exploration. When you are asking your partner to let go, do your best to let go as you facilitate your partners in releasing. You will find that this happens naturally if you are open to it. Refrain from leading, judging their responses, or giving them advice. Also refrain from discussing the explorations until you have both completed them and you have spent a few minutes in silence. Be sure to validate your partner's point of view, even if it does not agree with your own.

Please refrain from playing the role of counselor or therapist even if you're a trained counselor or therapist. If your partner brings up a medical condition that would ordinarily require a trained medical professional, recommend that they get whatever support they need in this area. If you are not sure whether or not they truly need medical support, you can recommend that they seek professional medical attention, just to be sure.

Have Group Share

Have volunteers from the group share what they got from the exercise. Make sure the group validates their perspective, and support them in letting go and moving up into greater freedom.

Sharing Gains

Give the group another opportunity to share gains if they choose.

Silence

Have the group spend a few minutes allowing their beingness to be in silence.

Thank Everyone for Coming

Thank everyone for coming and encourage the group to maintain the silence within as they go home or go about their day.

Gains from *Happiness is Free:* **Book I**

Please use the space on this page and the next to share your gains from working with this material. If you would prefer you can use a separate sheet of paper or e-mail us at **release@sedona.com** to send us your gains.

Gains from book 1 *continued*

_____

_____

_____

_____

_____

_____

_____

_____

_____

_____

I give Sedona Training Associates permission to quote my comments in promotional materials and future books. I understand that in exchange I am entitled to receive a discount on the Sedona Method® Course or the Holistic Releasing™ tape sets.

Signature _____

Name _____

Address _____

City, State _____ Zip or Postal Code _____

Phone _____

E-mail Address _____

WE ARE HERE FOR YOU

Sedona Training Associates is dedicated to helping you liberate your true nature and to have, be, and do all that you choose. Our products have been created for this purpose. To accelerate your progress, we highly encourage you to attend one of our live seminars or purchase a tape program. The following are some of our offerings.

The Sedona Method® Course,

both as a live seminar or as our home study audio program, will show you how to elegantly and easily tap your natural ability to let go of any unwanted thought or feeling on the spot. In addition to gaining deeper awareness of the ultimate truth and your natural state of unlimited happiness, the Sedona Method® can free you to have any or all of the following: more money, better relationships, more radiant health and well being, more effective goal achievement, plus how to break bad habits and other self-sabotaging behaviors, lose weight, stop smoking, and sleep better.

You will also be able to easily, effortlessly and joyously free yourself from stress, tension, panic, fear, anxiety, depression, indecision, low self-esteem and self-doubt, fatigue, insomnia, co-dependency, uncontrolled anger, and grief. In short, you will enjoy living a happier, more productive, more satisfying, more loving and happy life.

The Holistic Releasing™ process, as you have probably already experienced from reading this book, can also accomplish all of the above. It is an integral part of our advanced seminars. You can also deepen your experience of this powerful tool by exploring our Holistic Releasing™ tape programs *Absolute Freedom* and *Practical Freedom.*

Absolute Freedom: This audio set utilizes Holistic Releasing™ to help you to easily recognize and dissolve the barriers that you imagine are keeping you from perceiving your true nature. These recordings will help you to discover the natural state of Beingness that has always been available to you here and now. You will discover that who you are has only appeared to be hidden by your self-imposed sense of limitation. You have always been absolutely free.

Practical Freedom: This audio set is designed to help you to rediscover the freedom to have, be, or do whatever you choose as an alive and practical part of your everyday life. It will help free you to perform at your best in every situation, and live your life with greater ease and clarity. As you apply Holistic Releasing™, you will find that even long-standing challenges dissolve and are replaced by a greater sense of mastery.